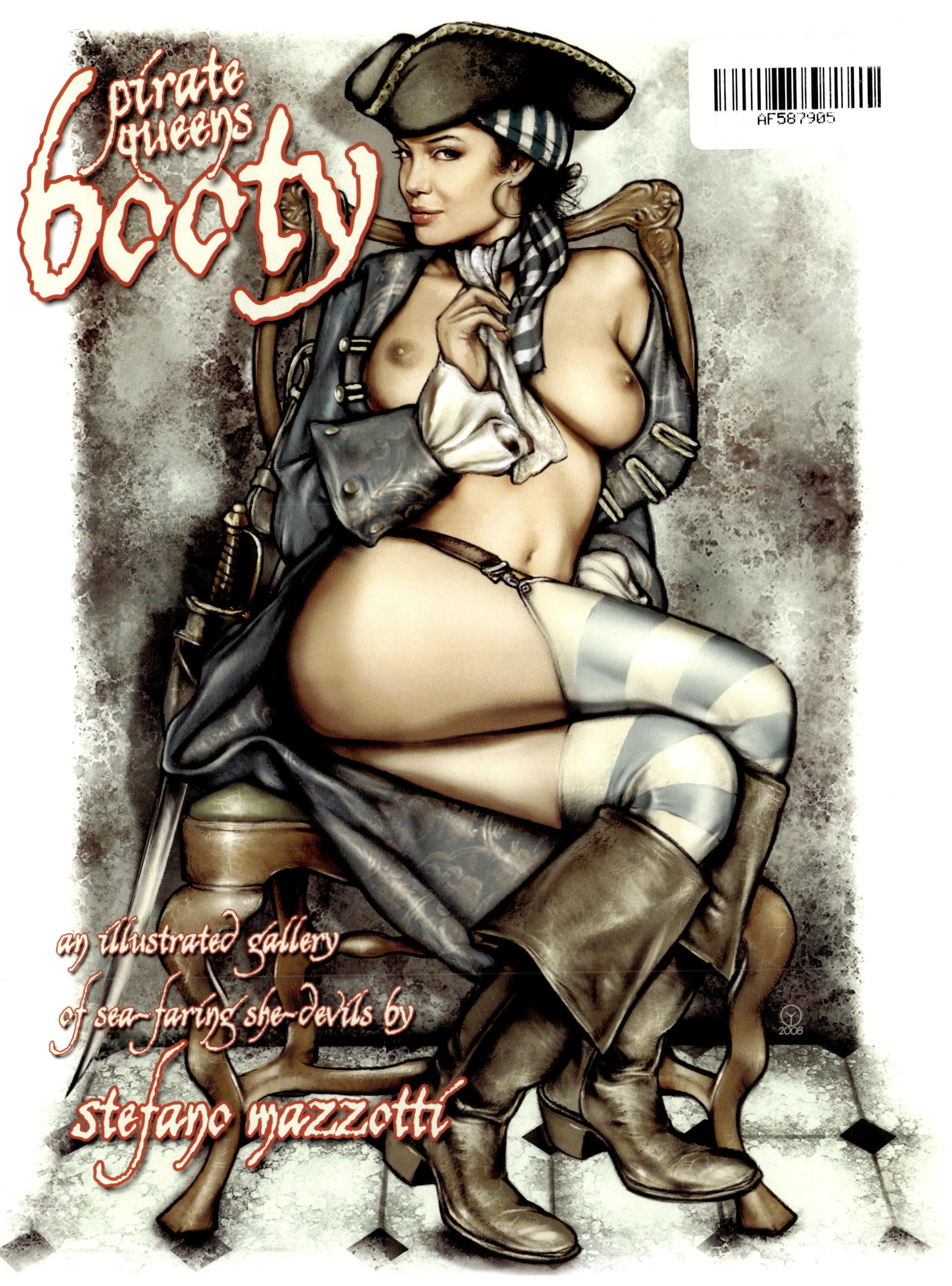
pirate queens
booty
an illustrated gallery
of sea-faring she-devils by
stefano mazzotti
2008
AF587905

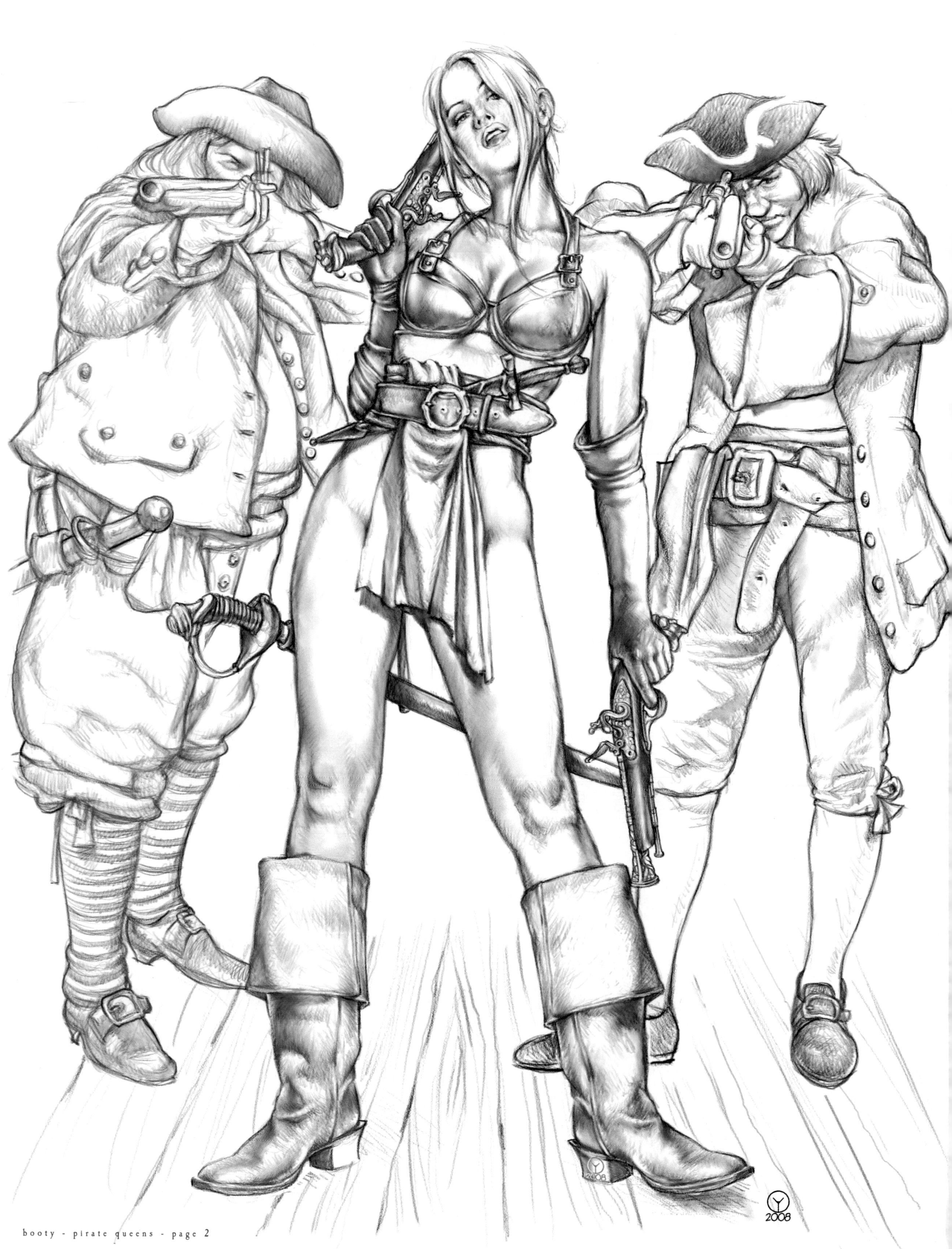

booty - pirate queens - page 2

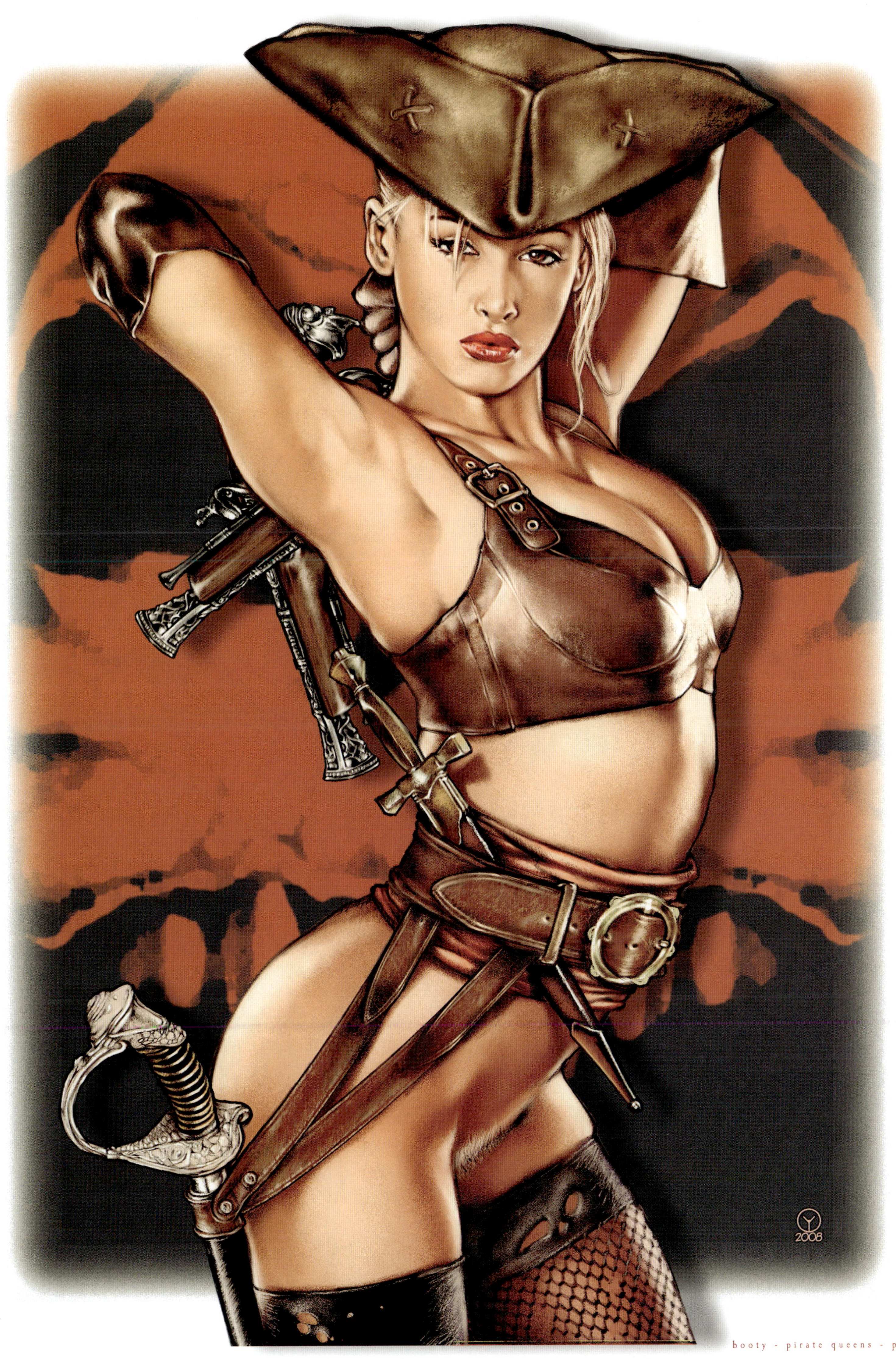
2008

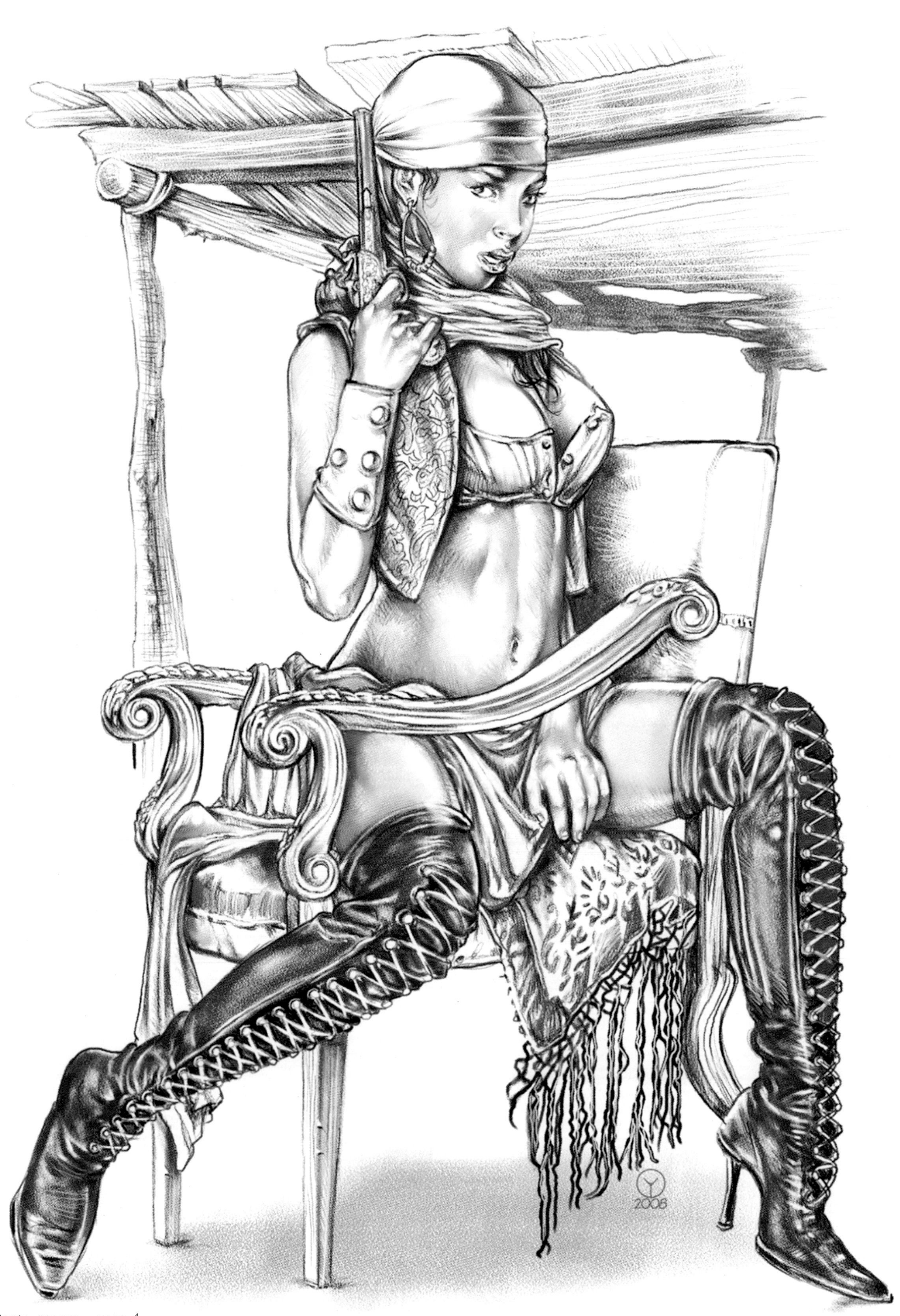
2008

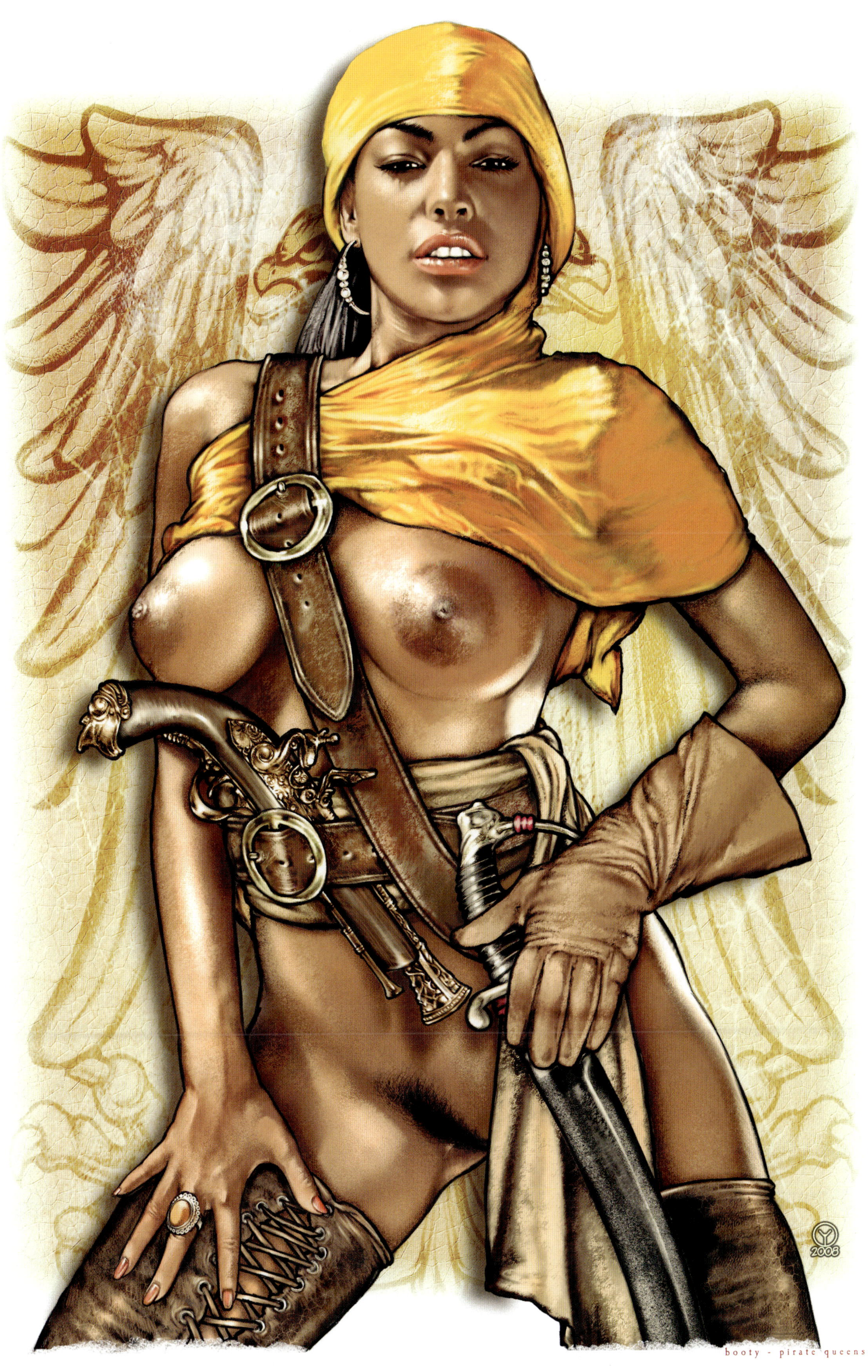
2008

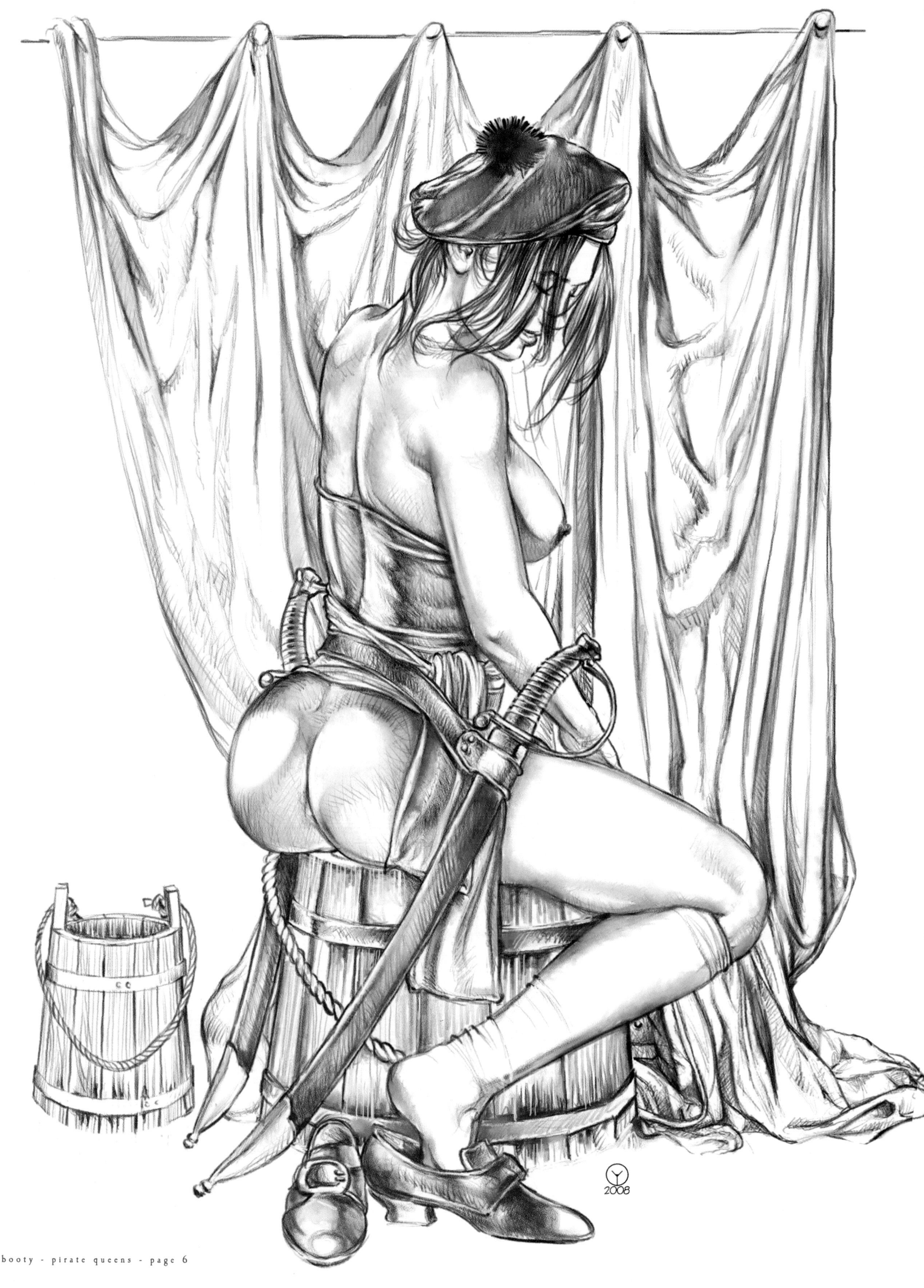
2008

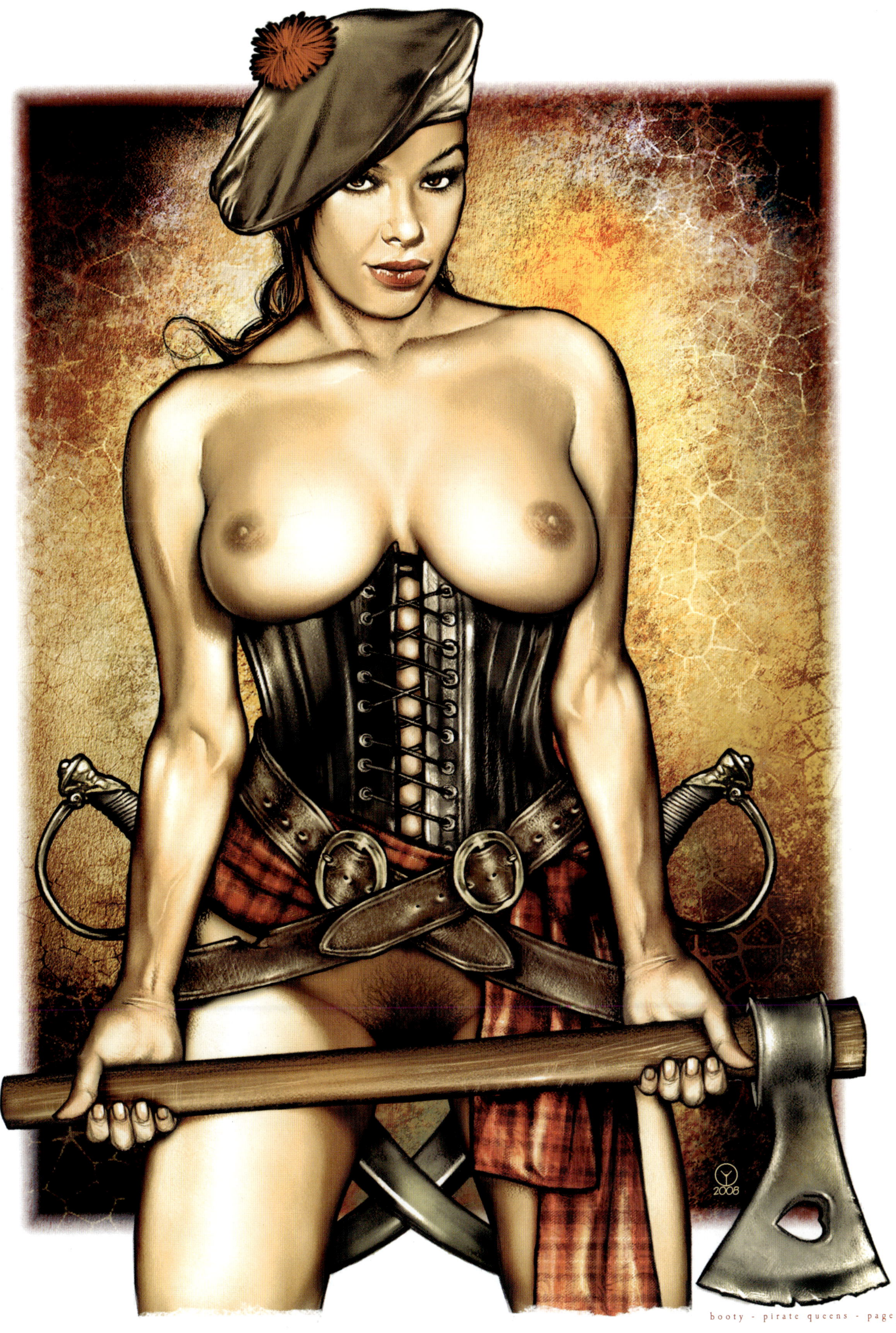
2008

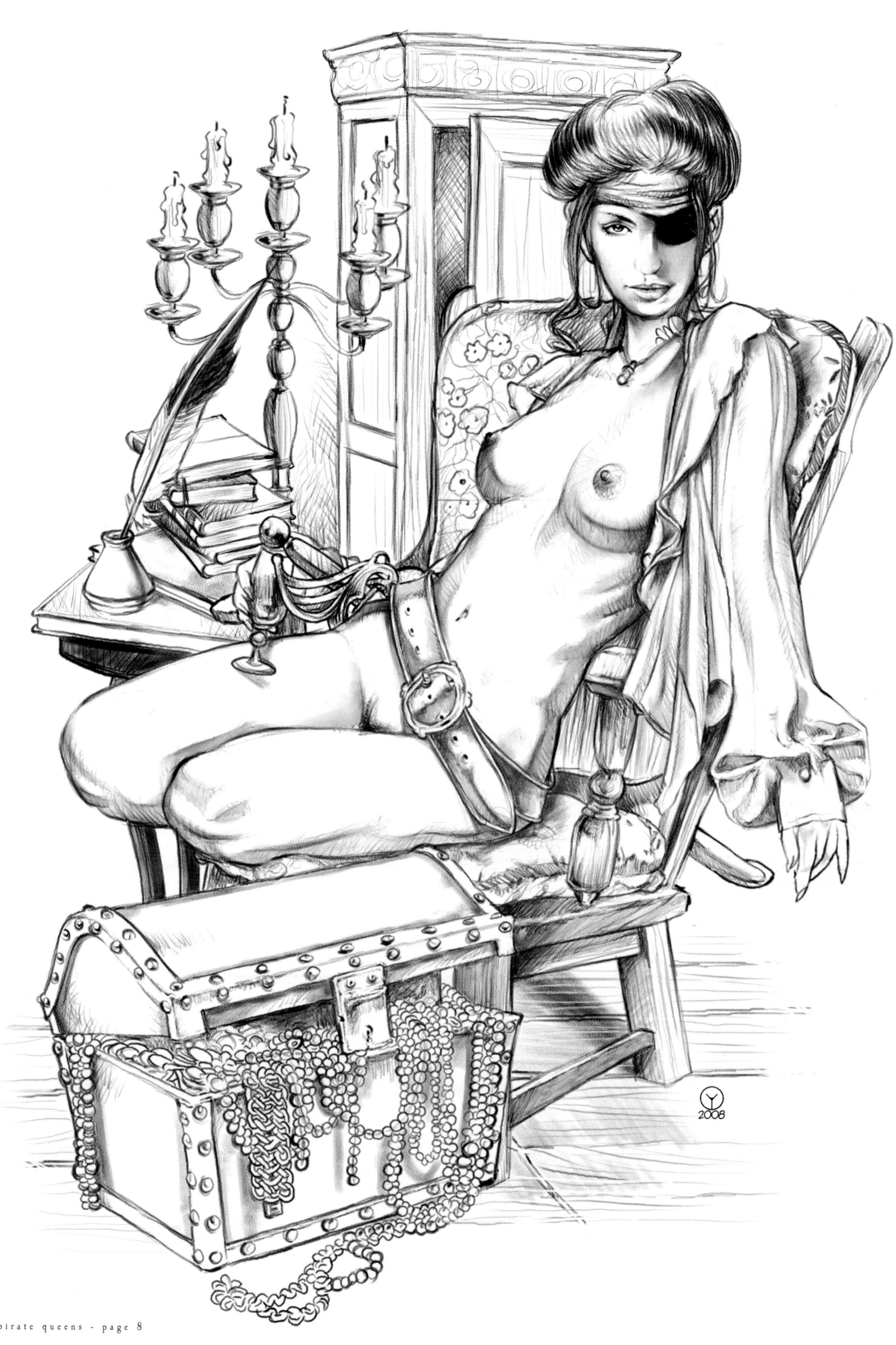
2008

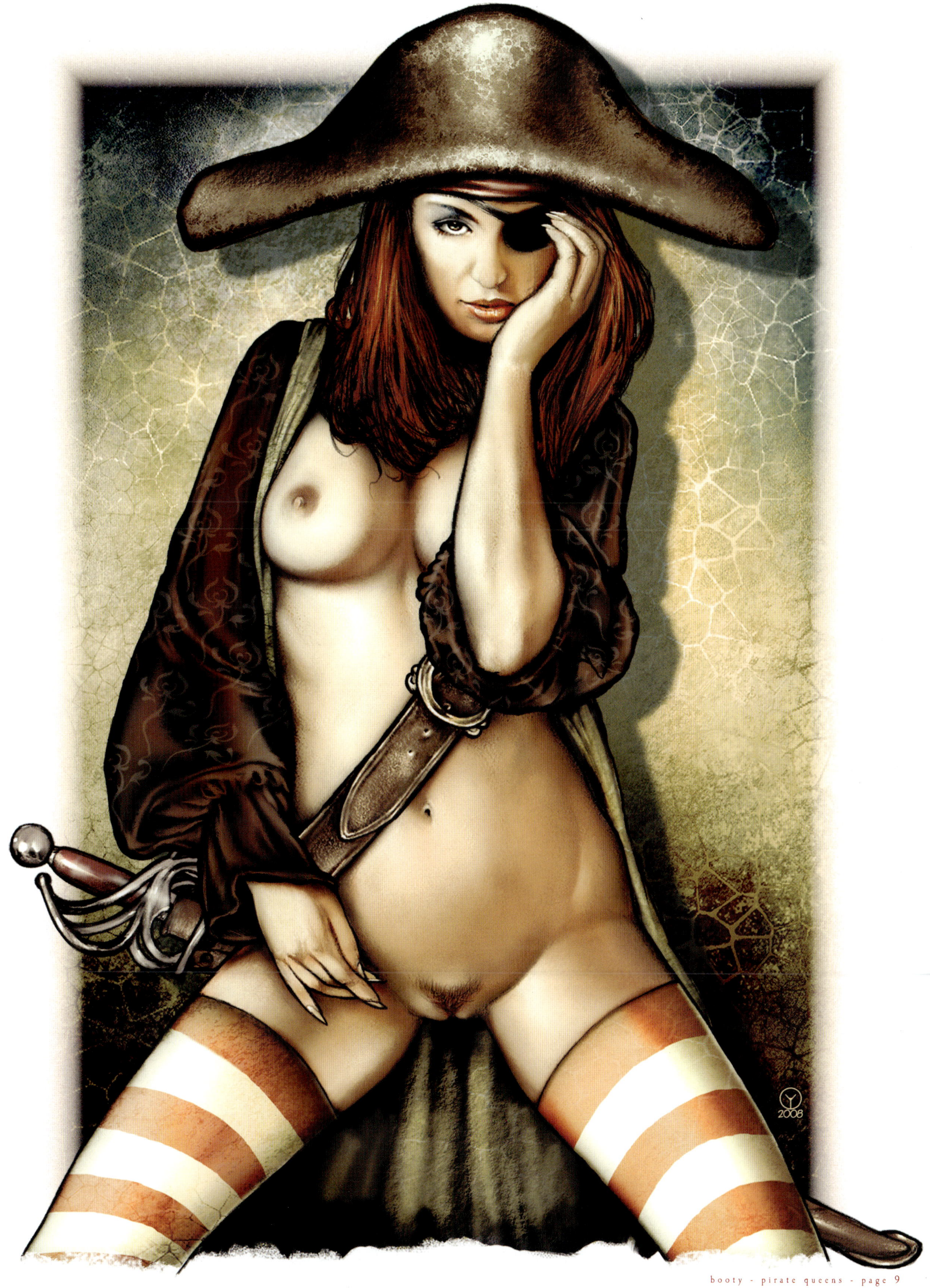
2008

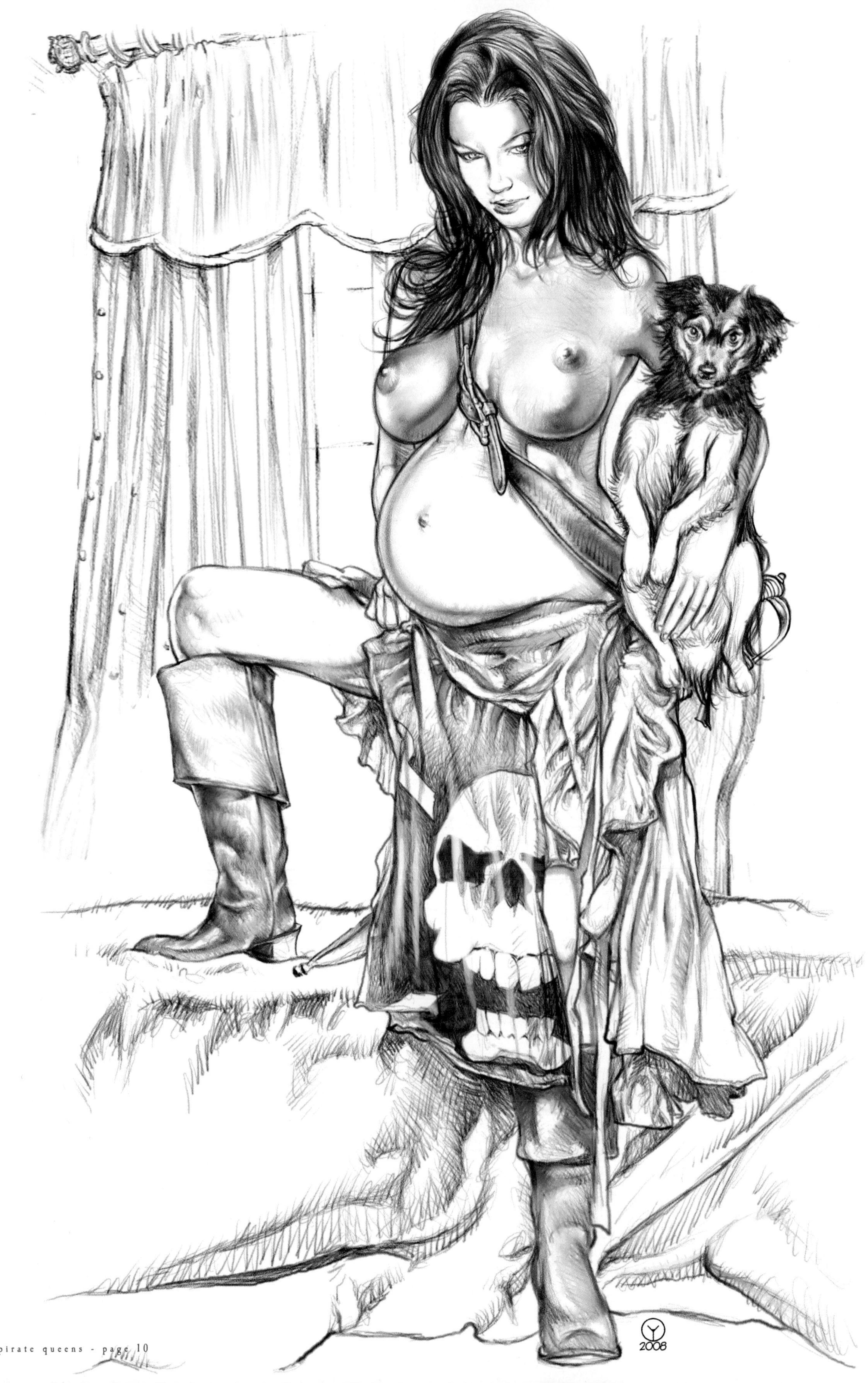
2008

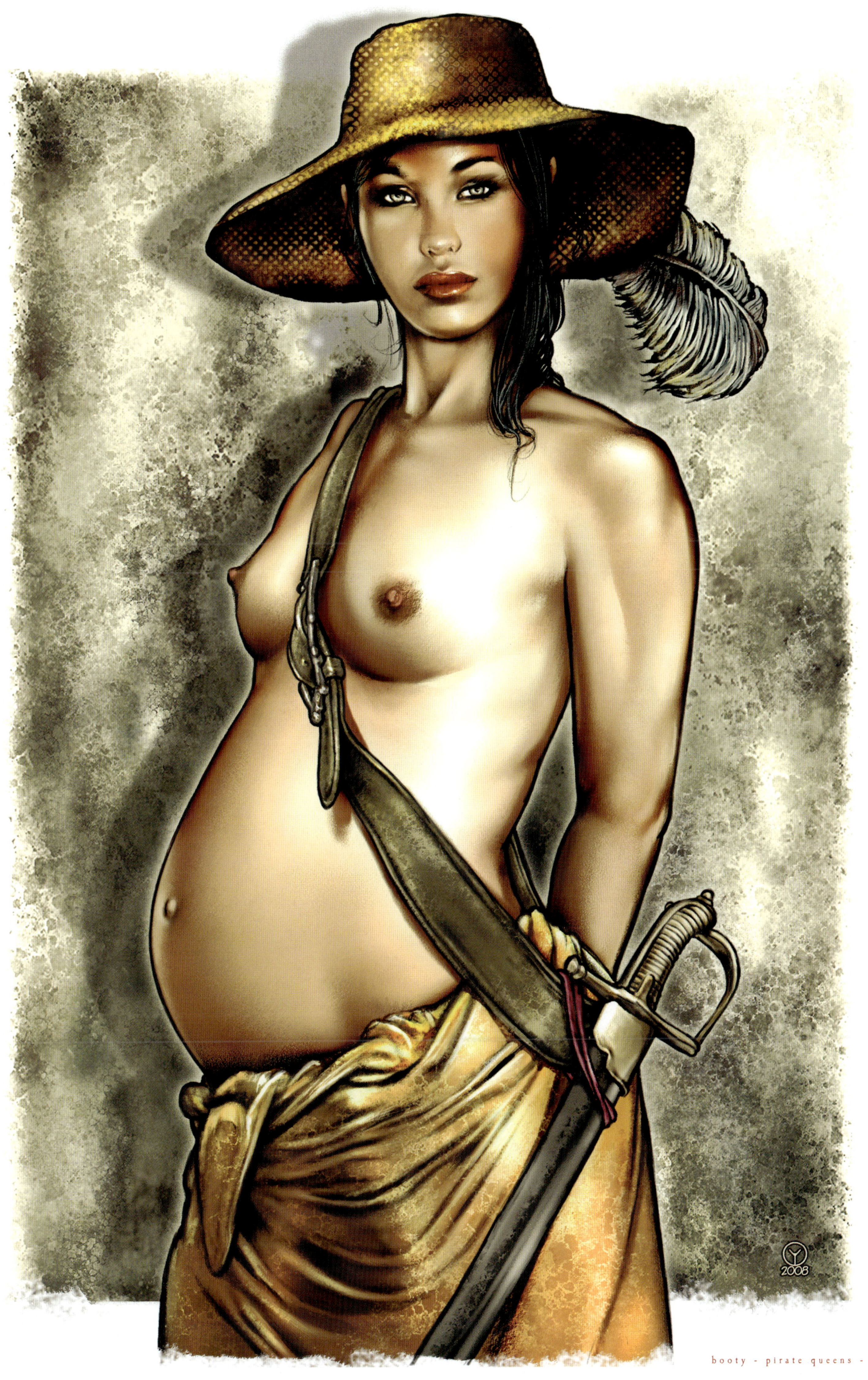
2008

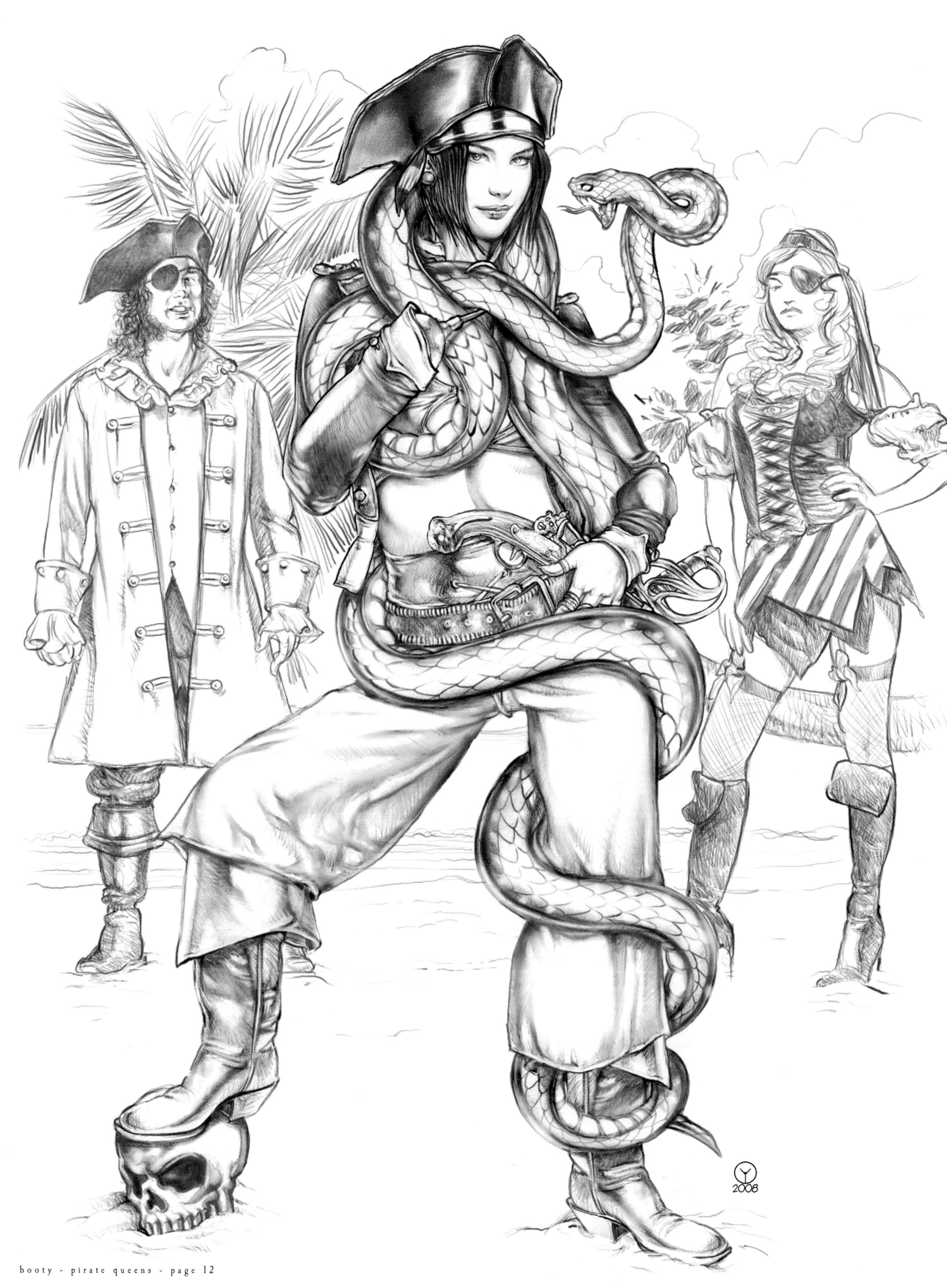
2008

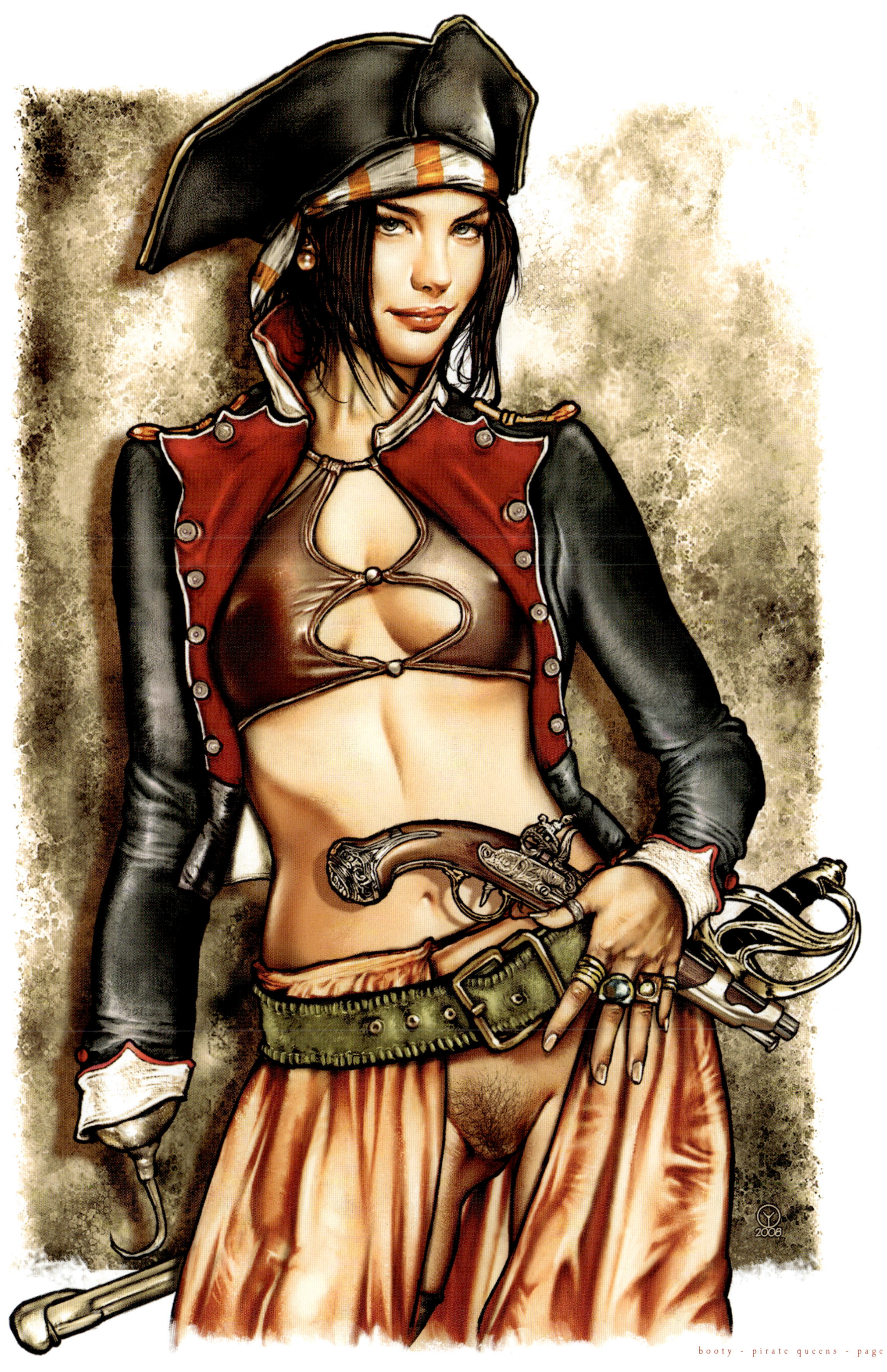
2008

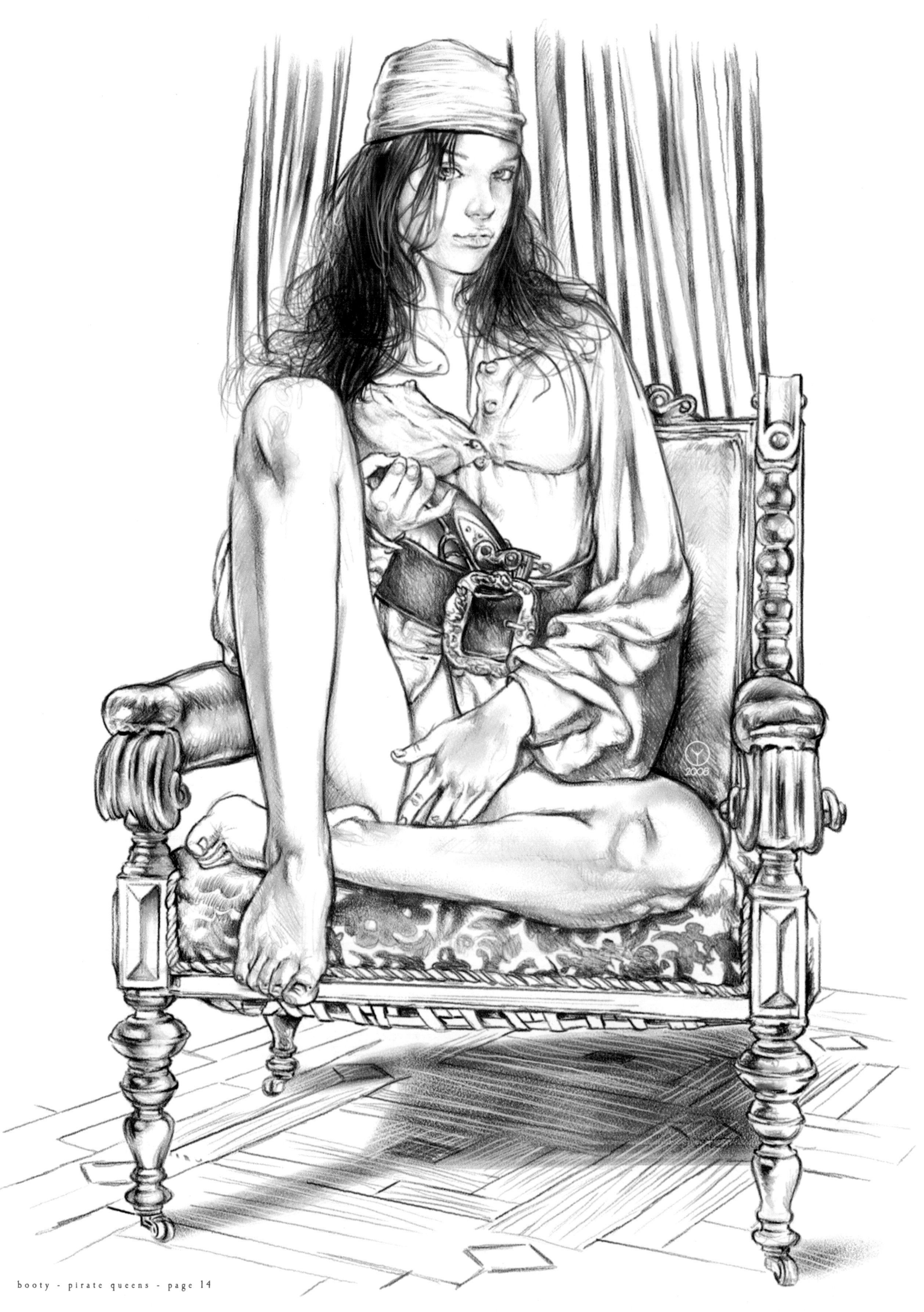
2006

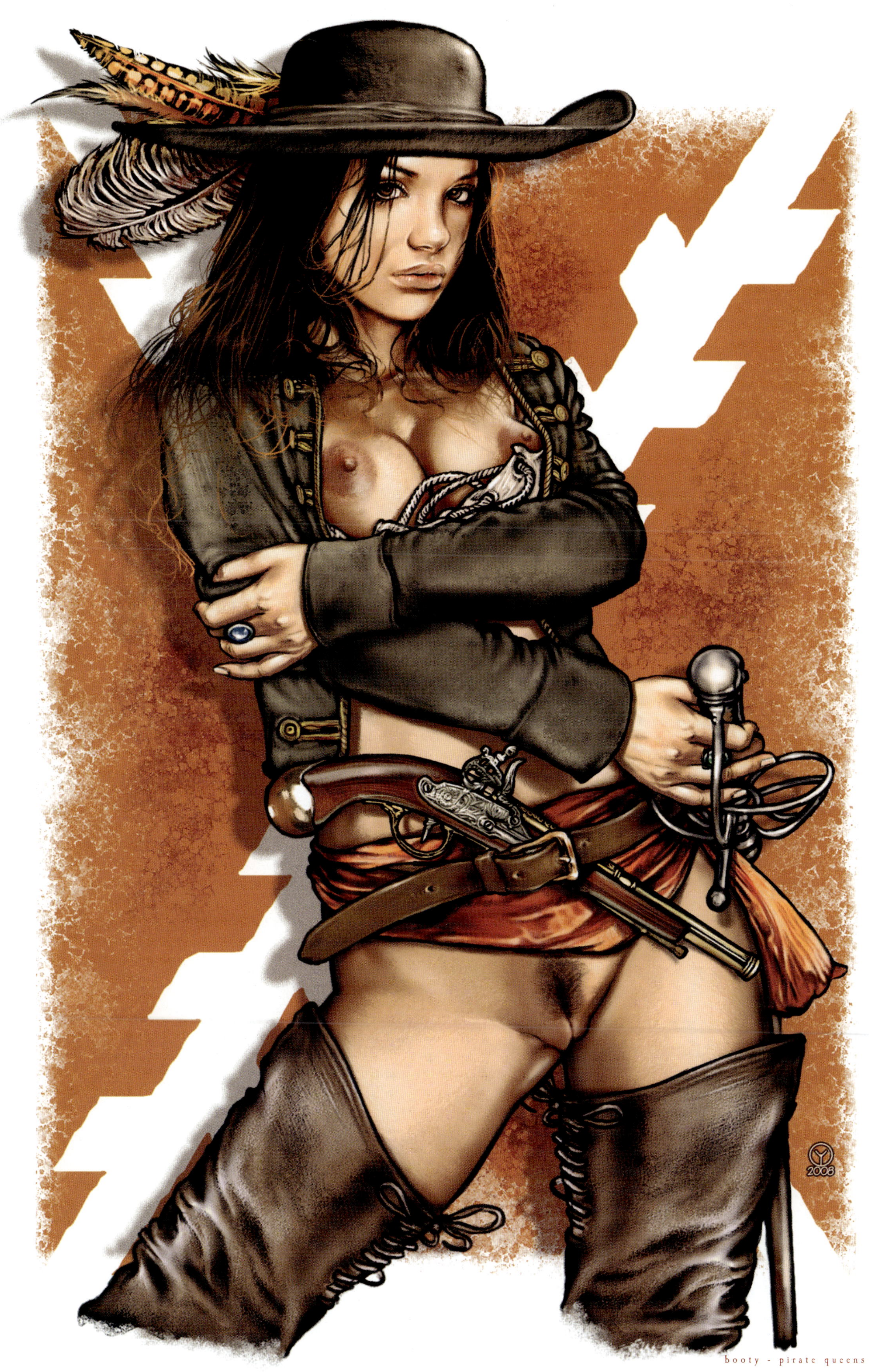

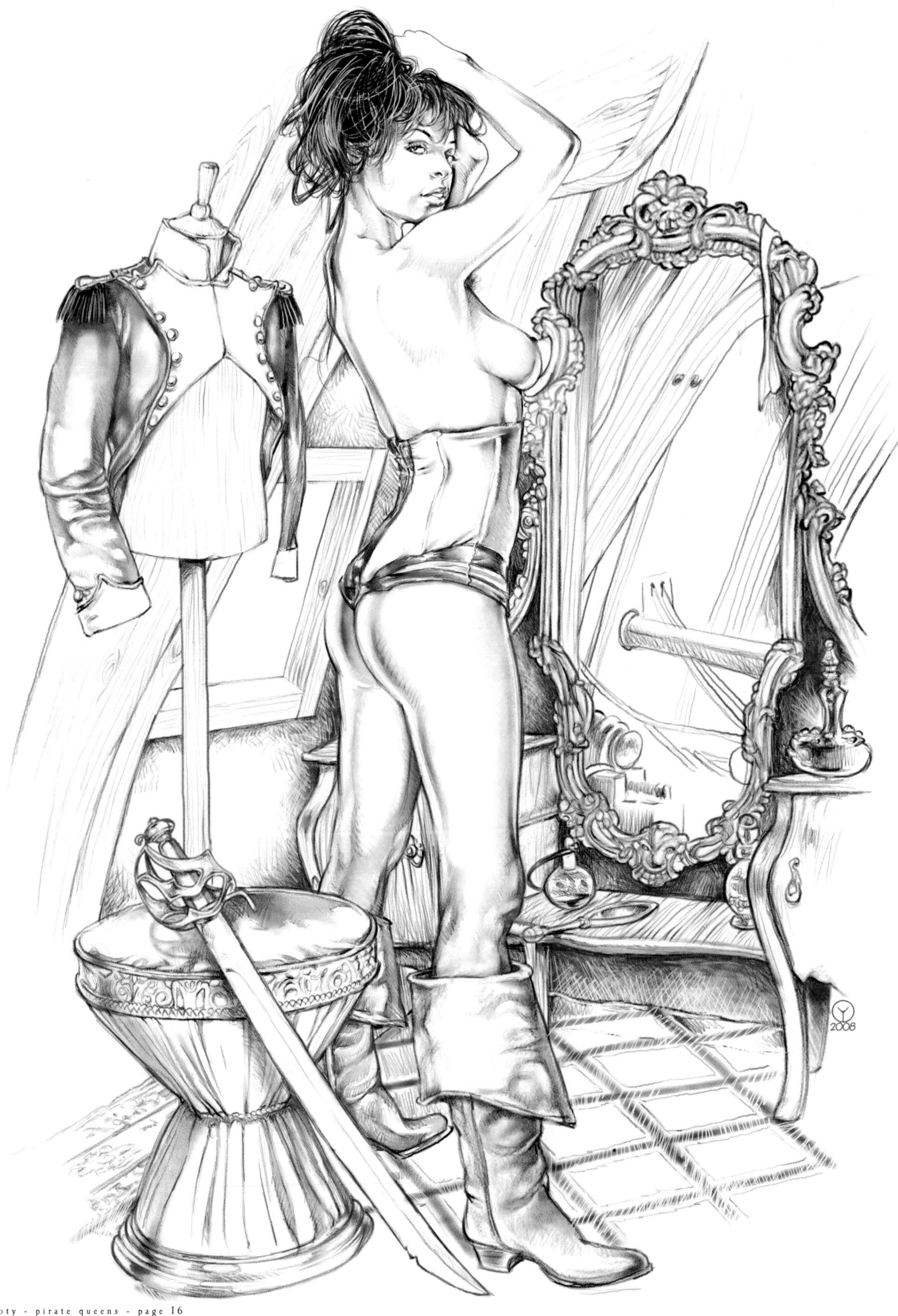
2008

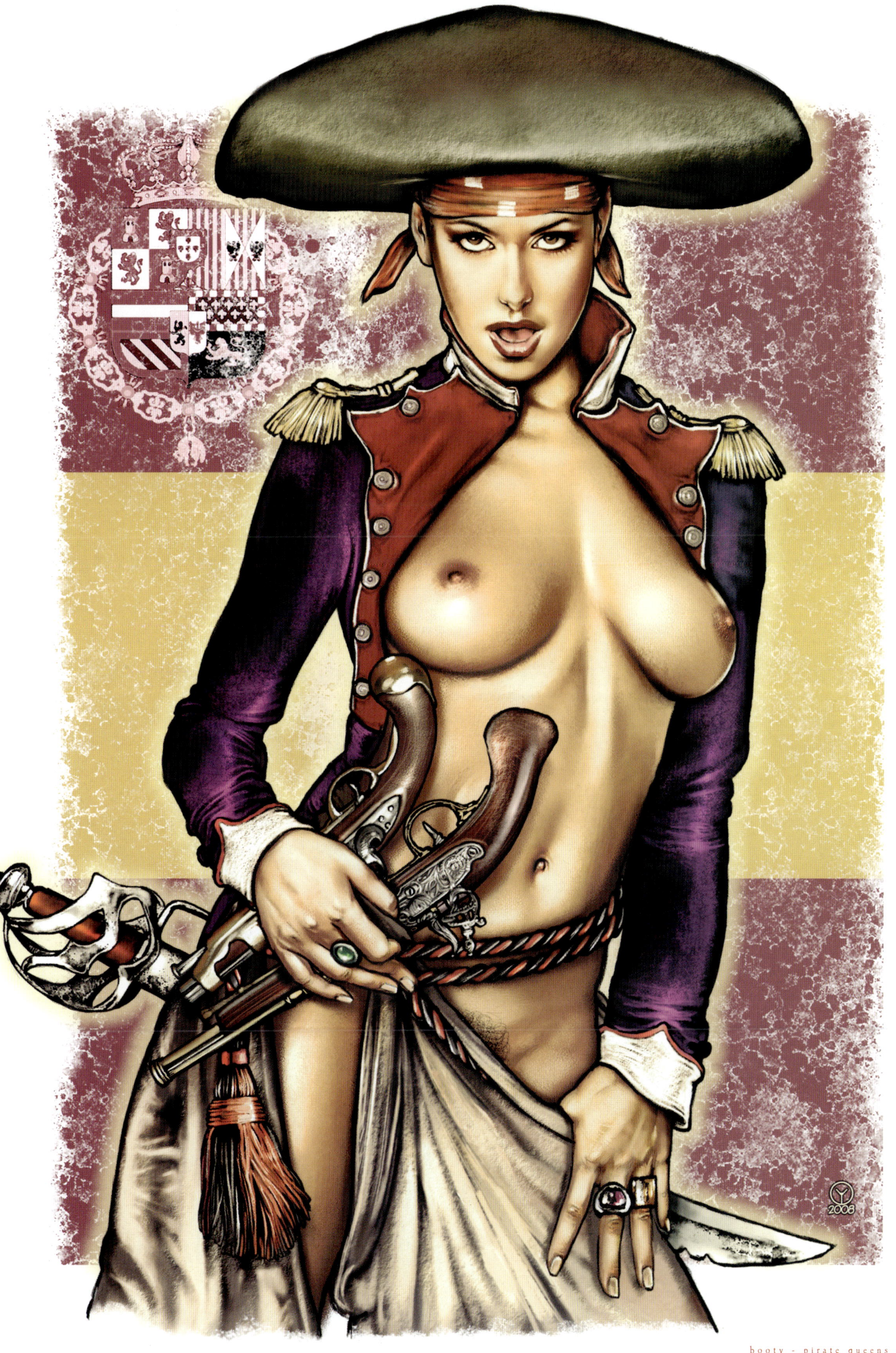

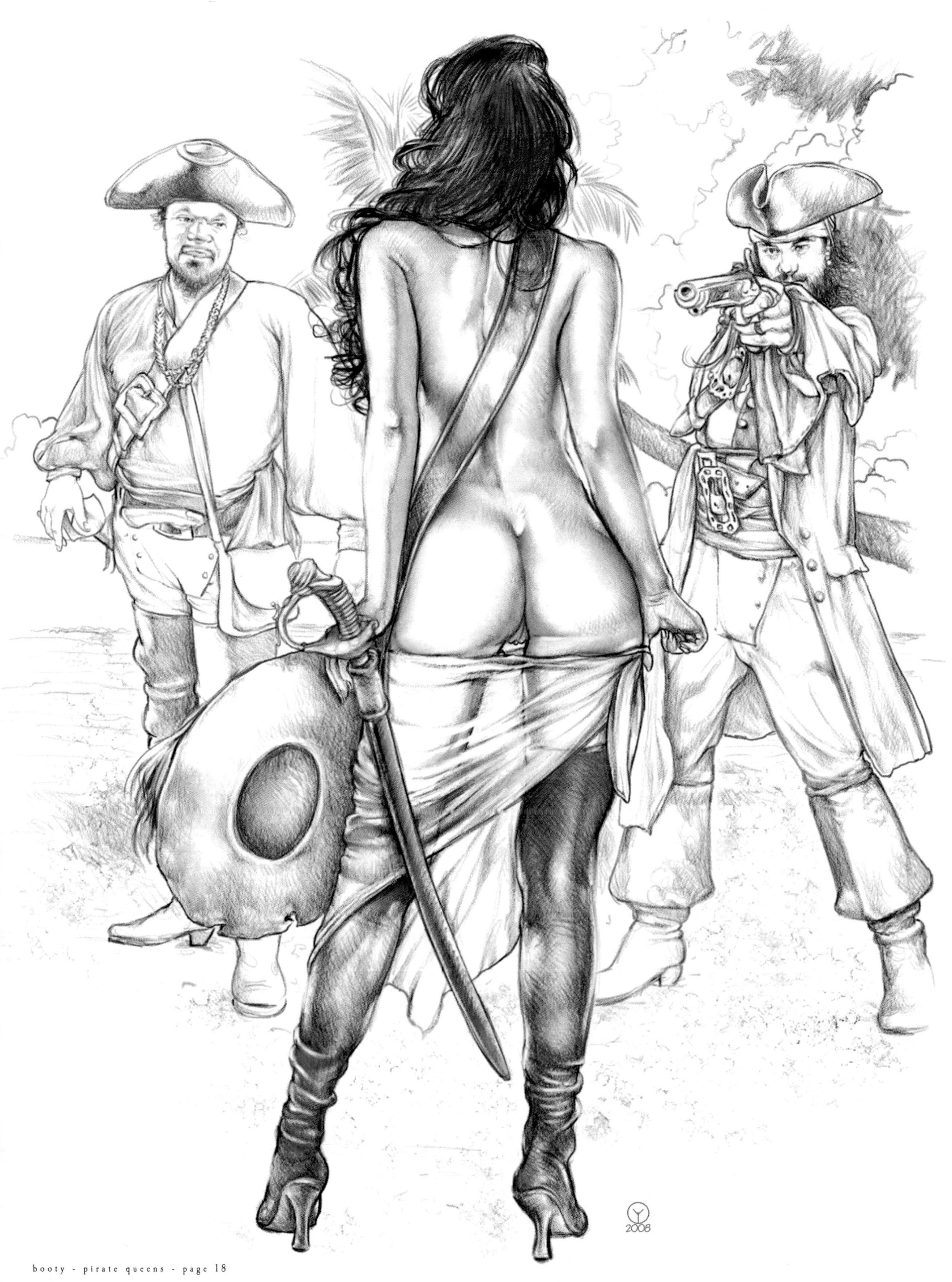
2008

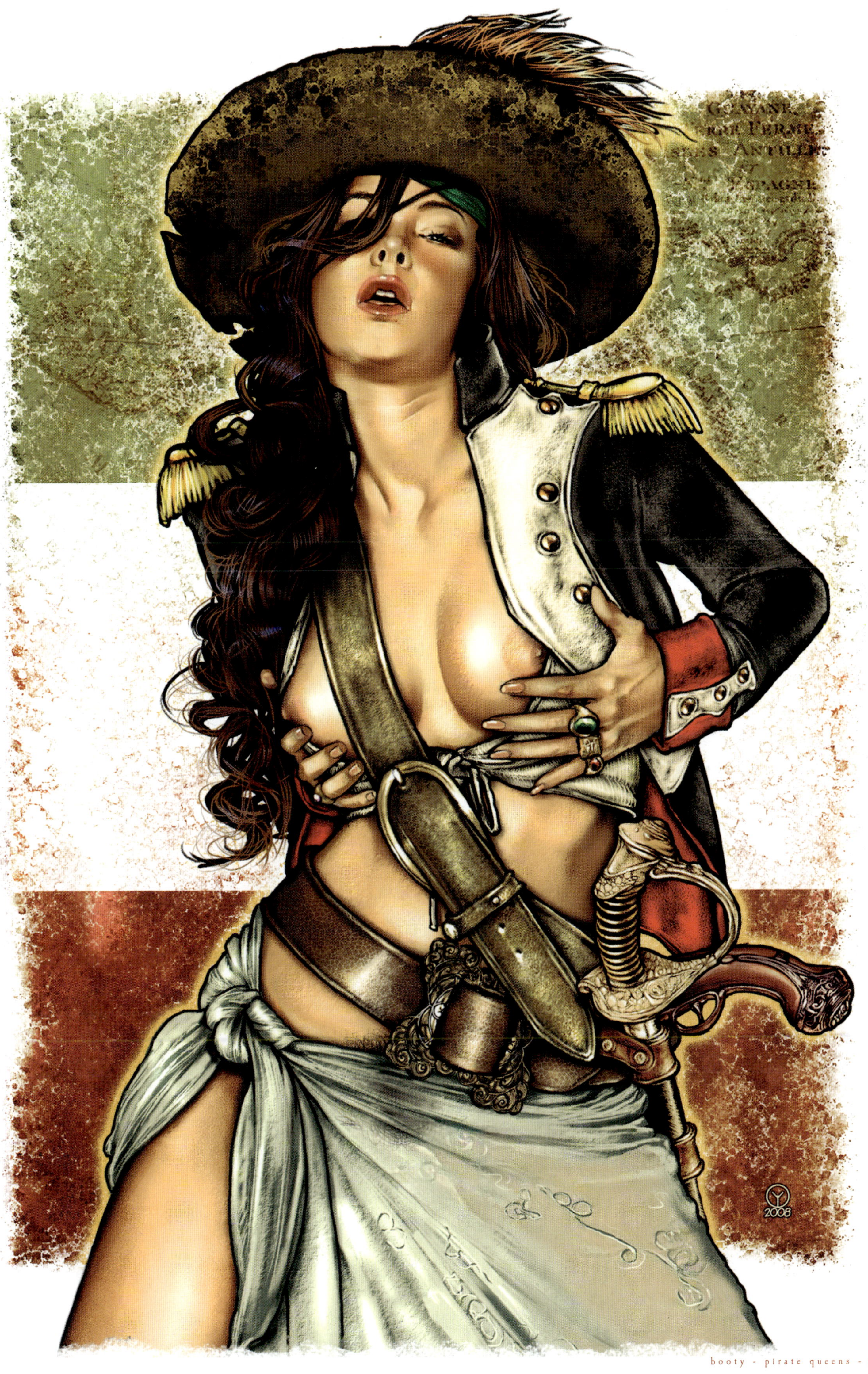

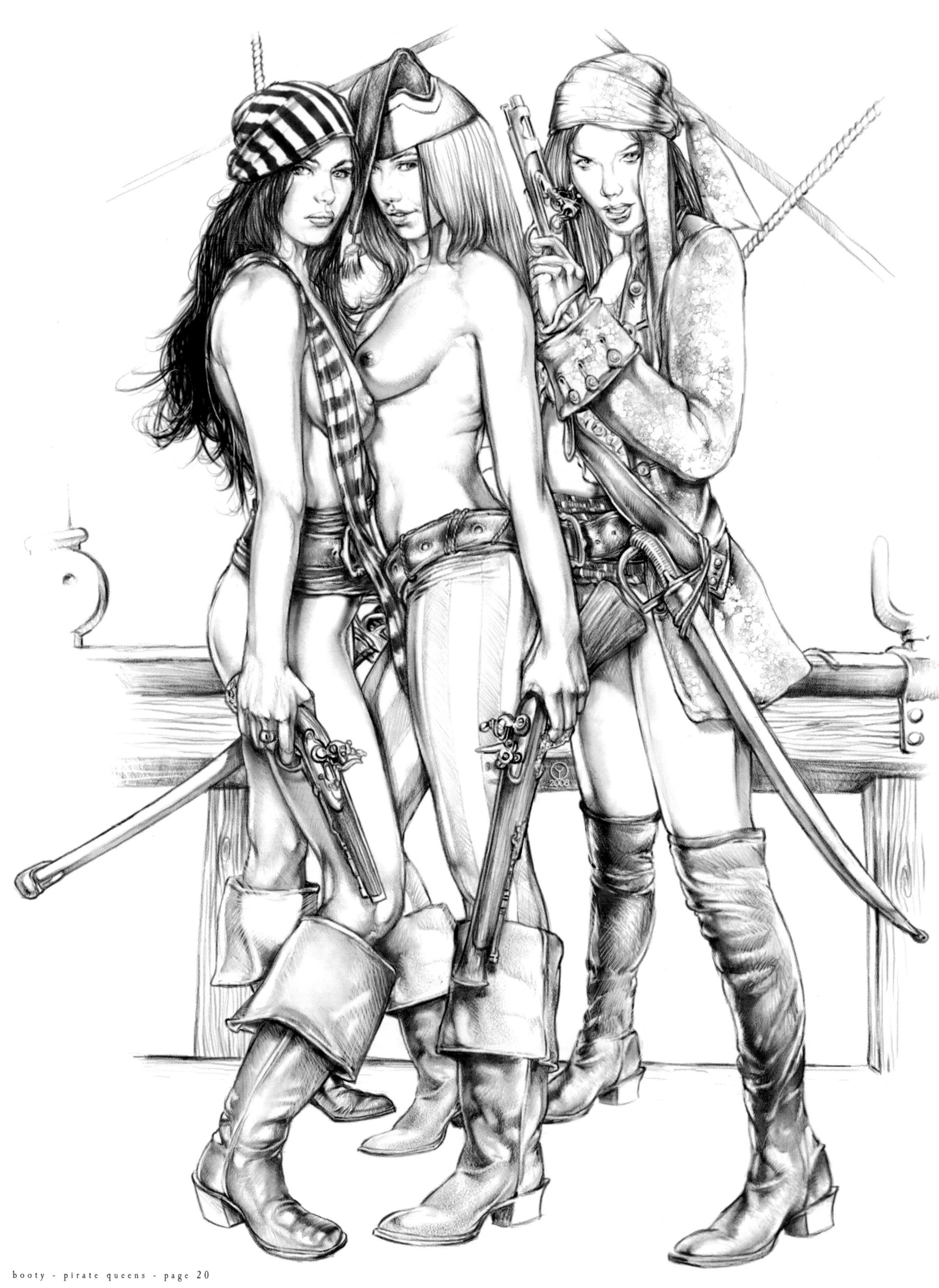

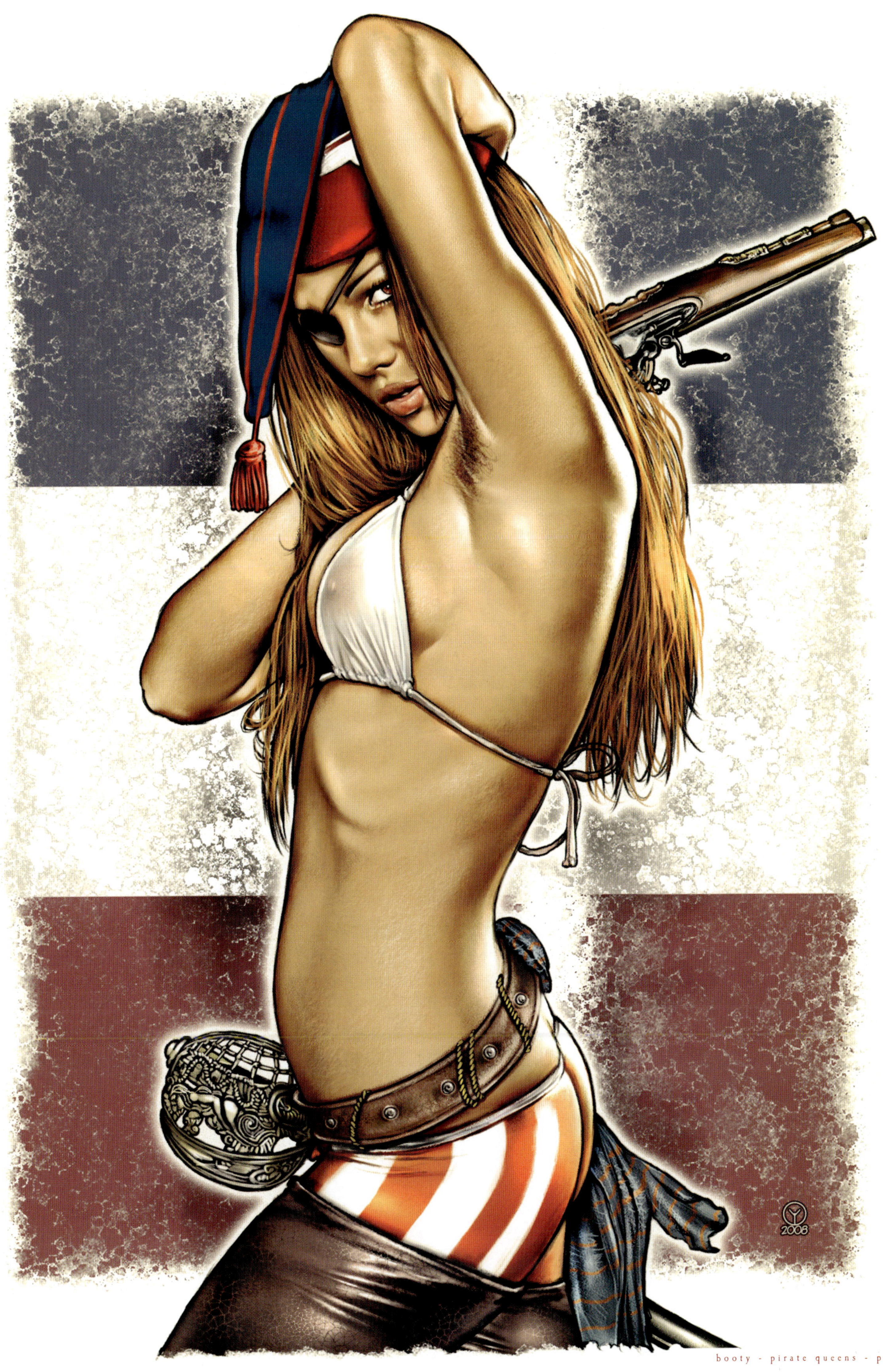
2008

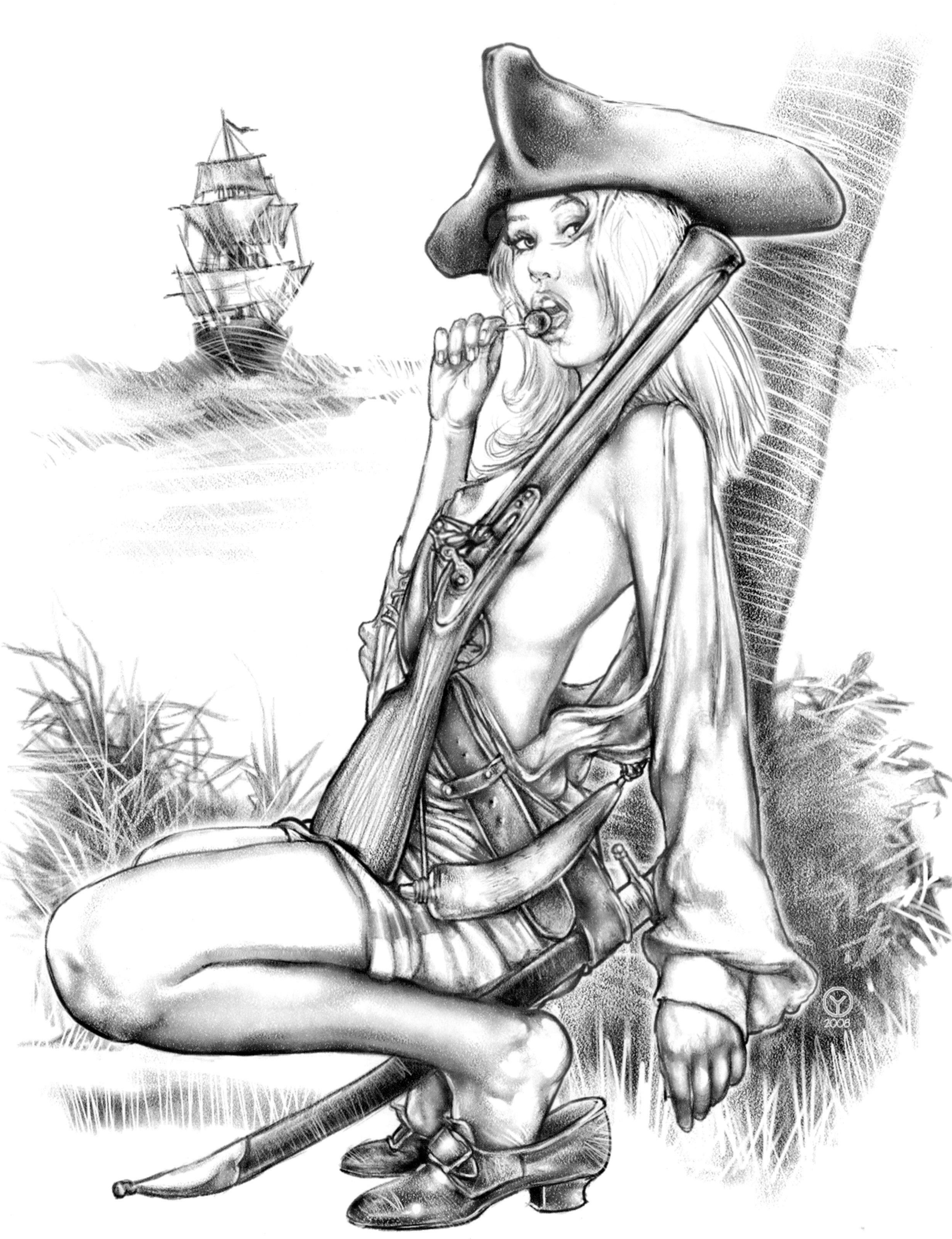
2008

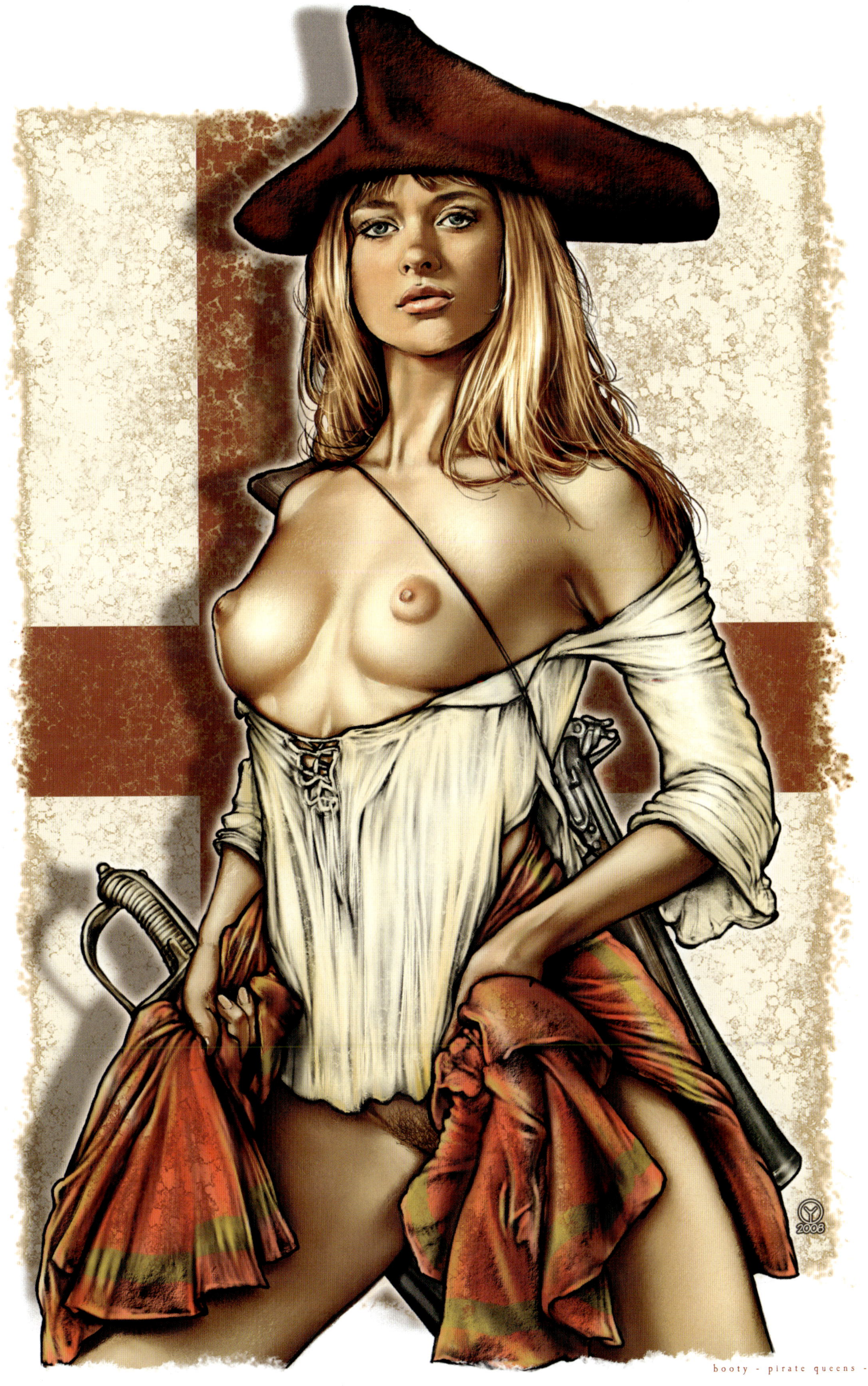
2008

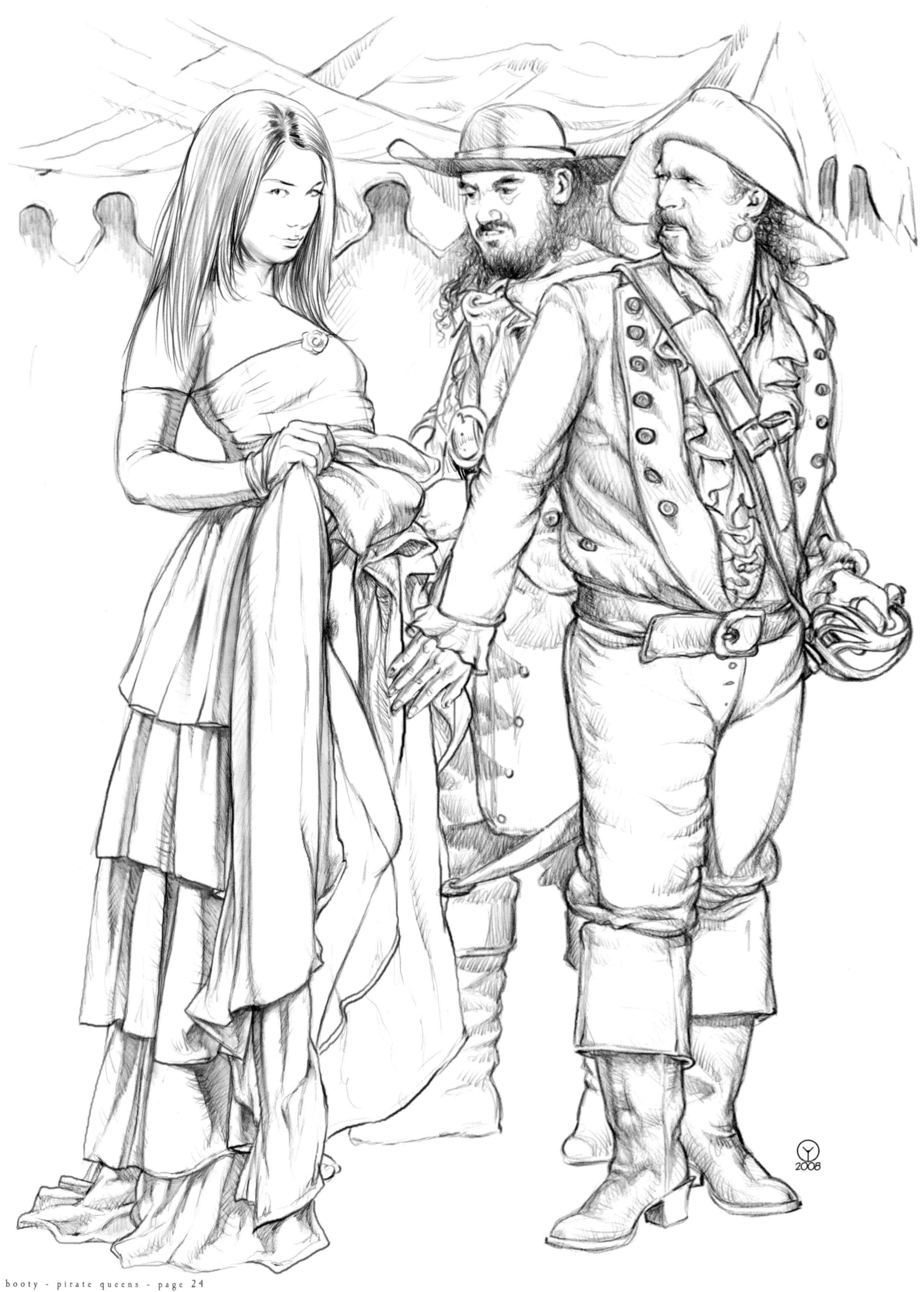
2008

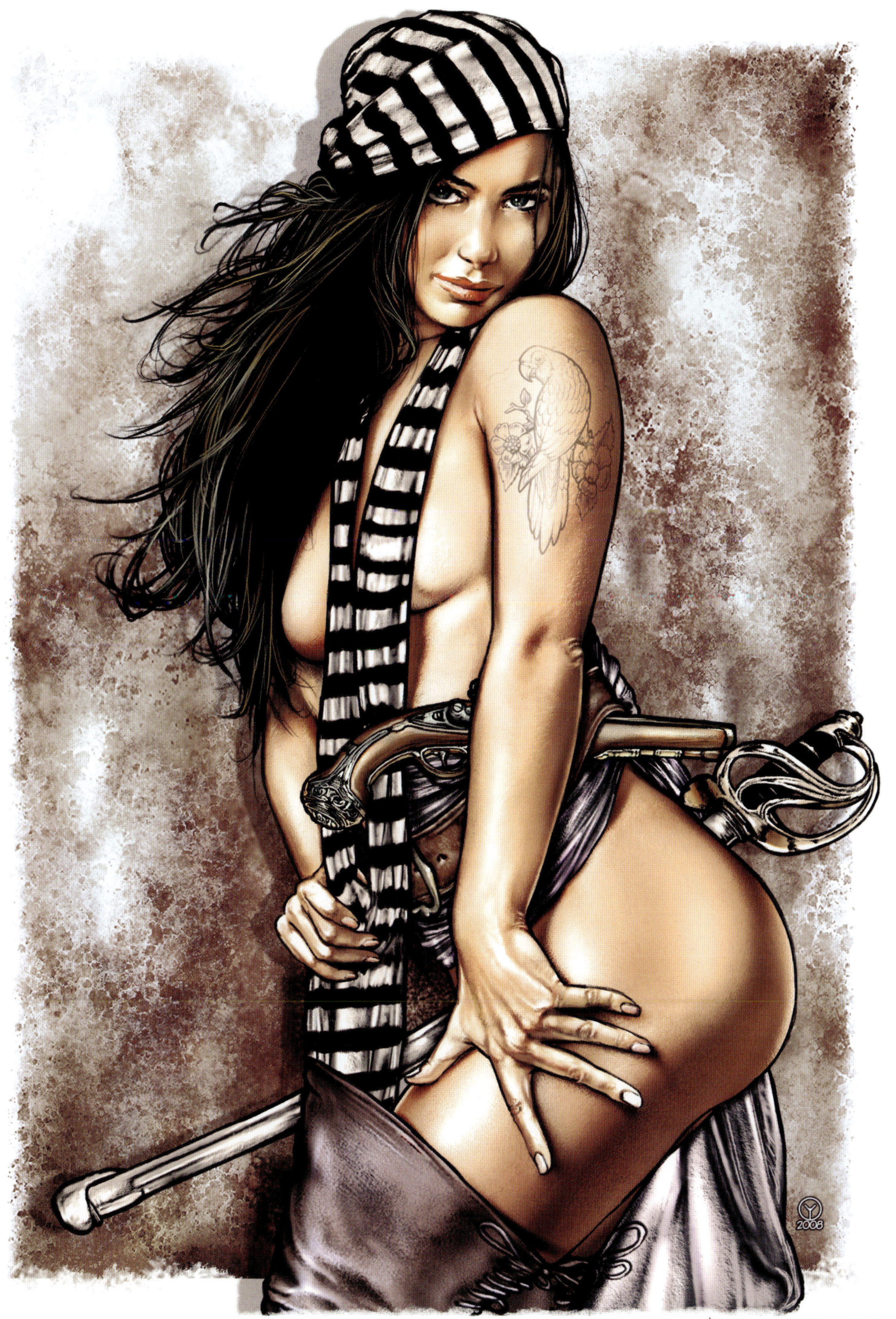
2008

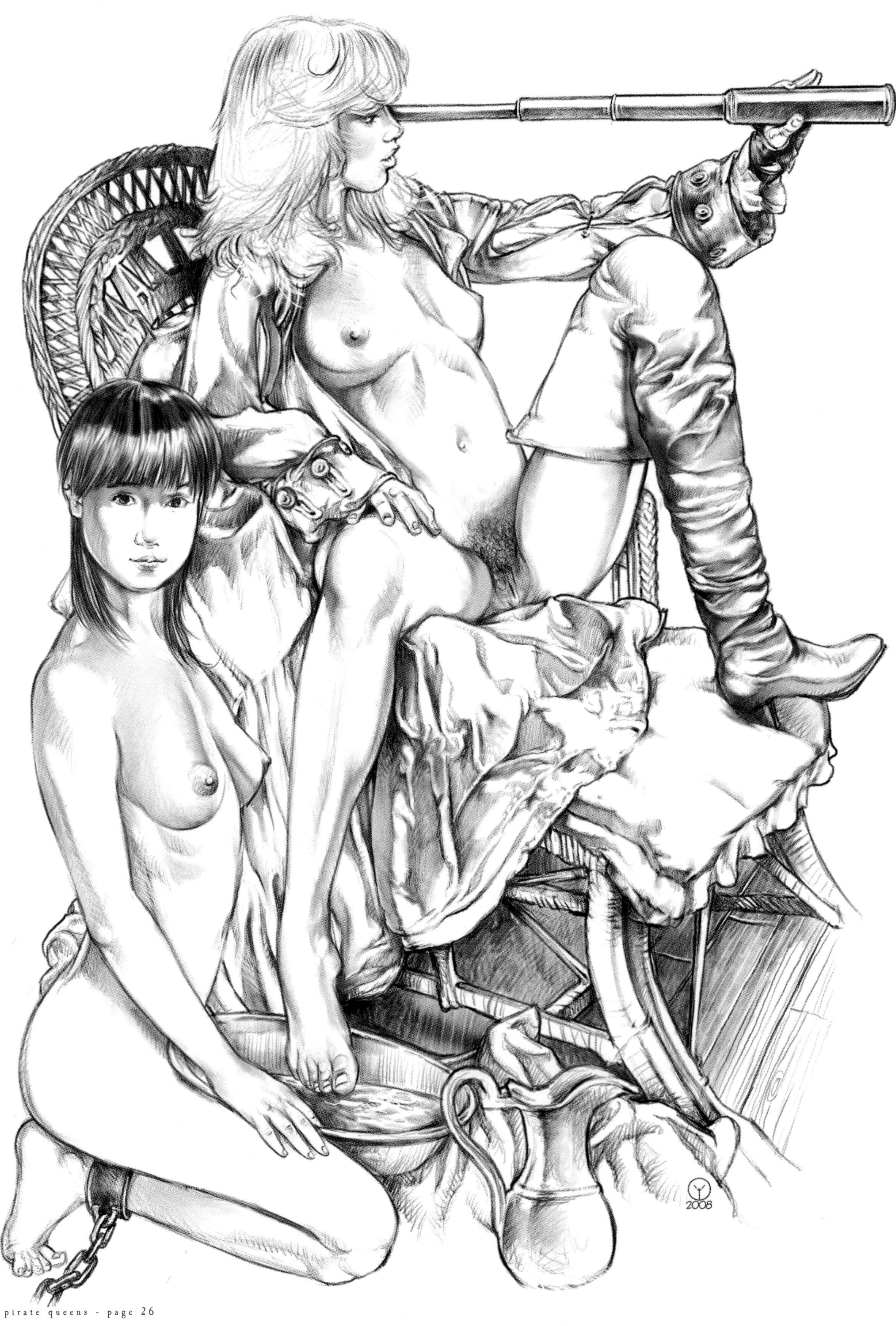
2008

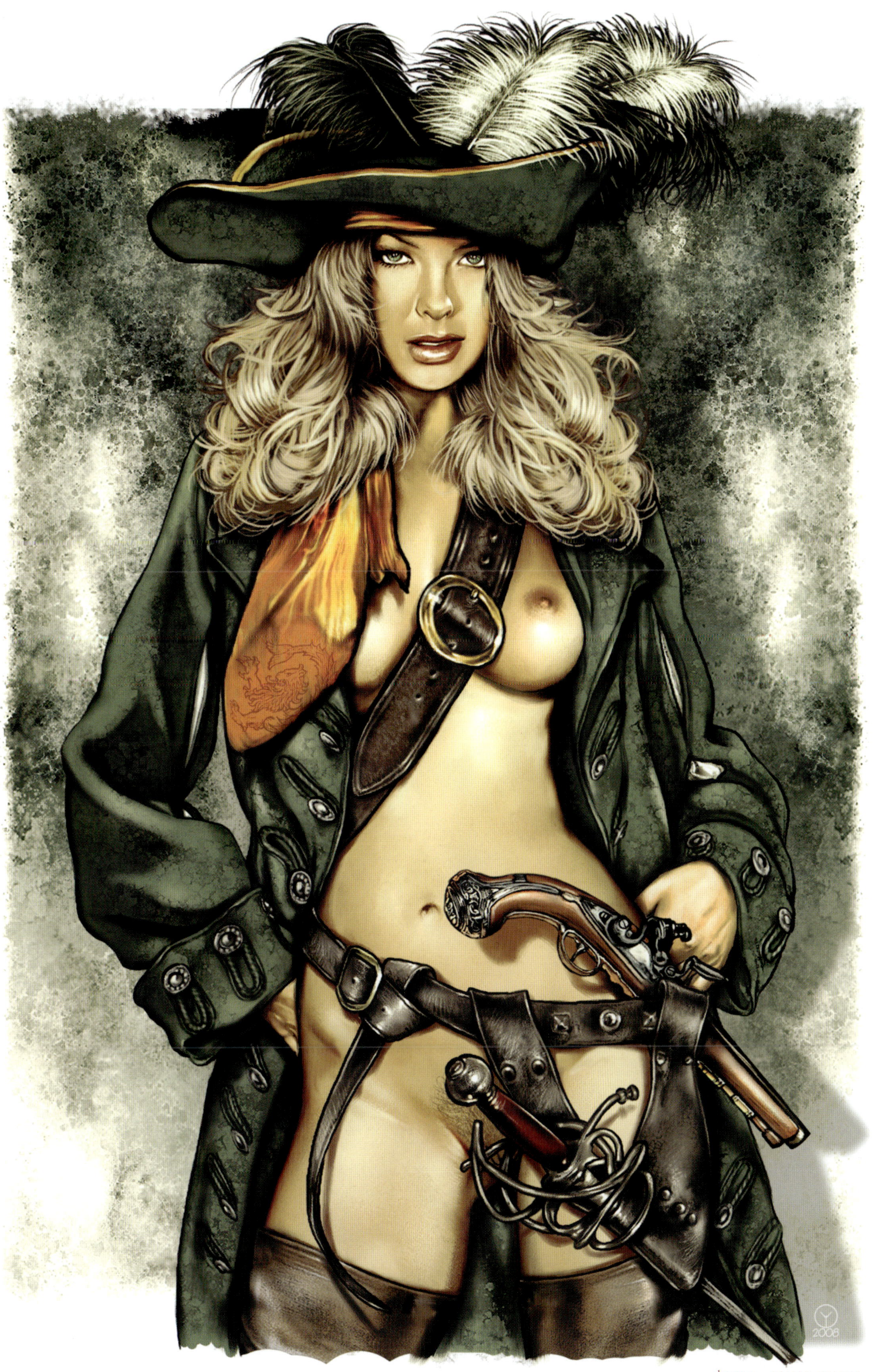

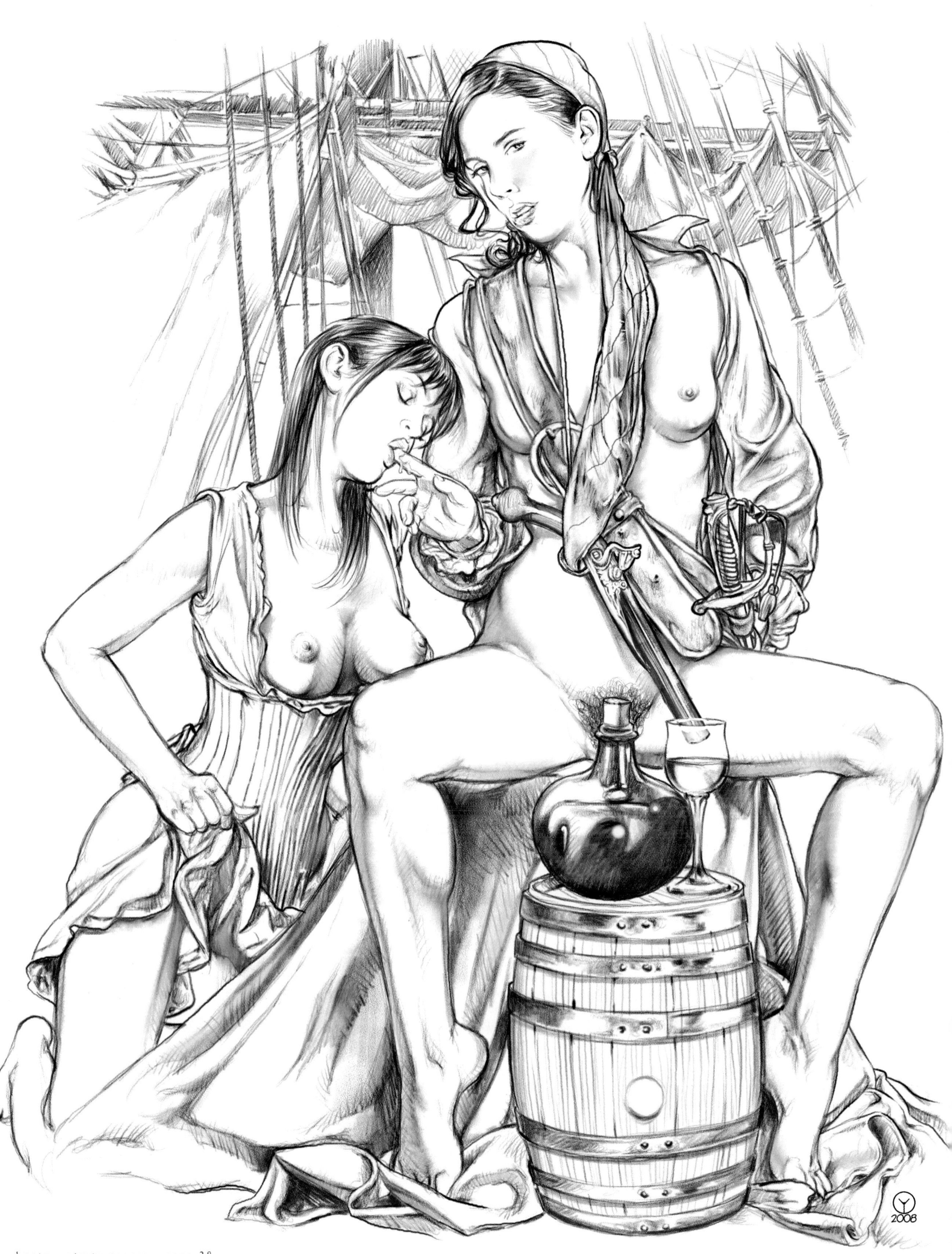
2008

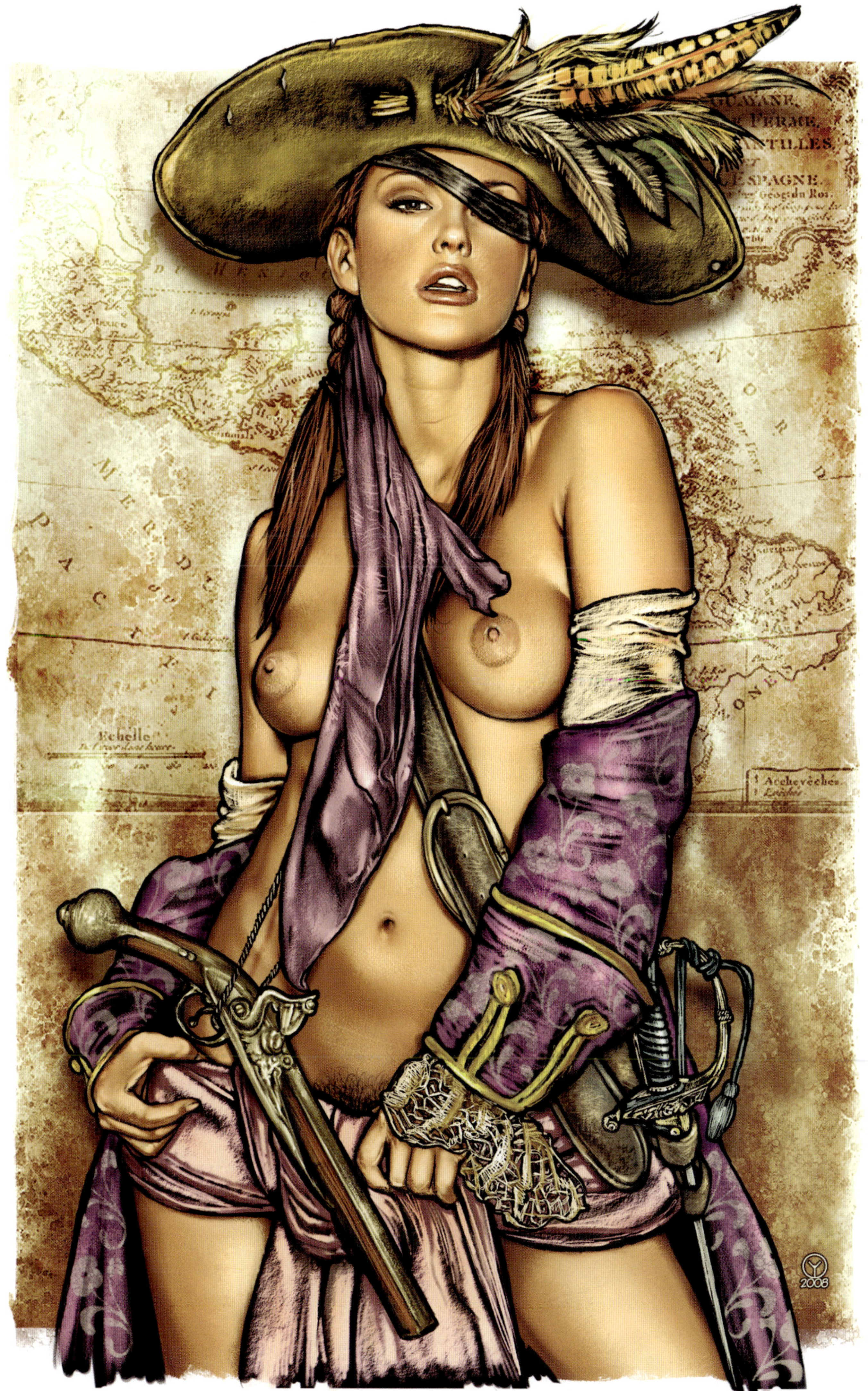
Echelle
2008

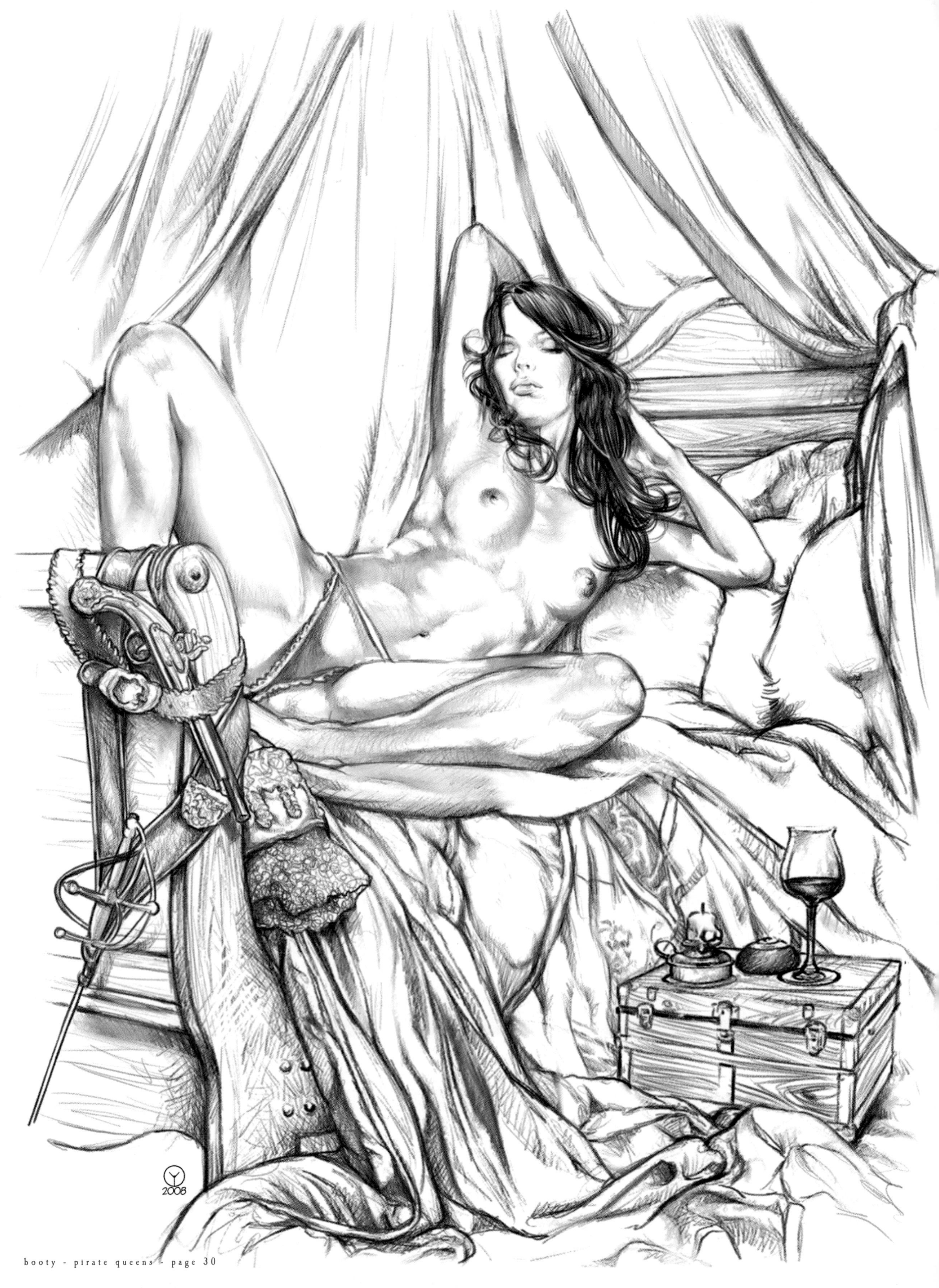
2008

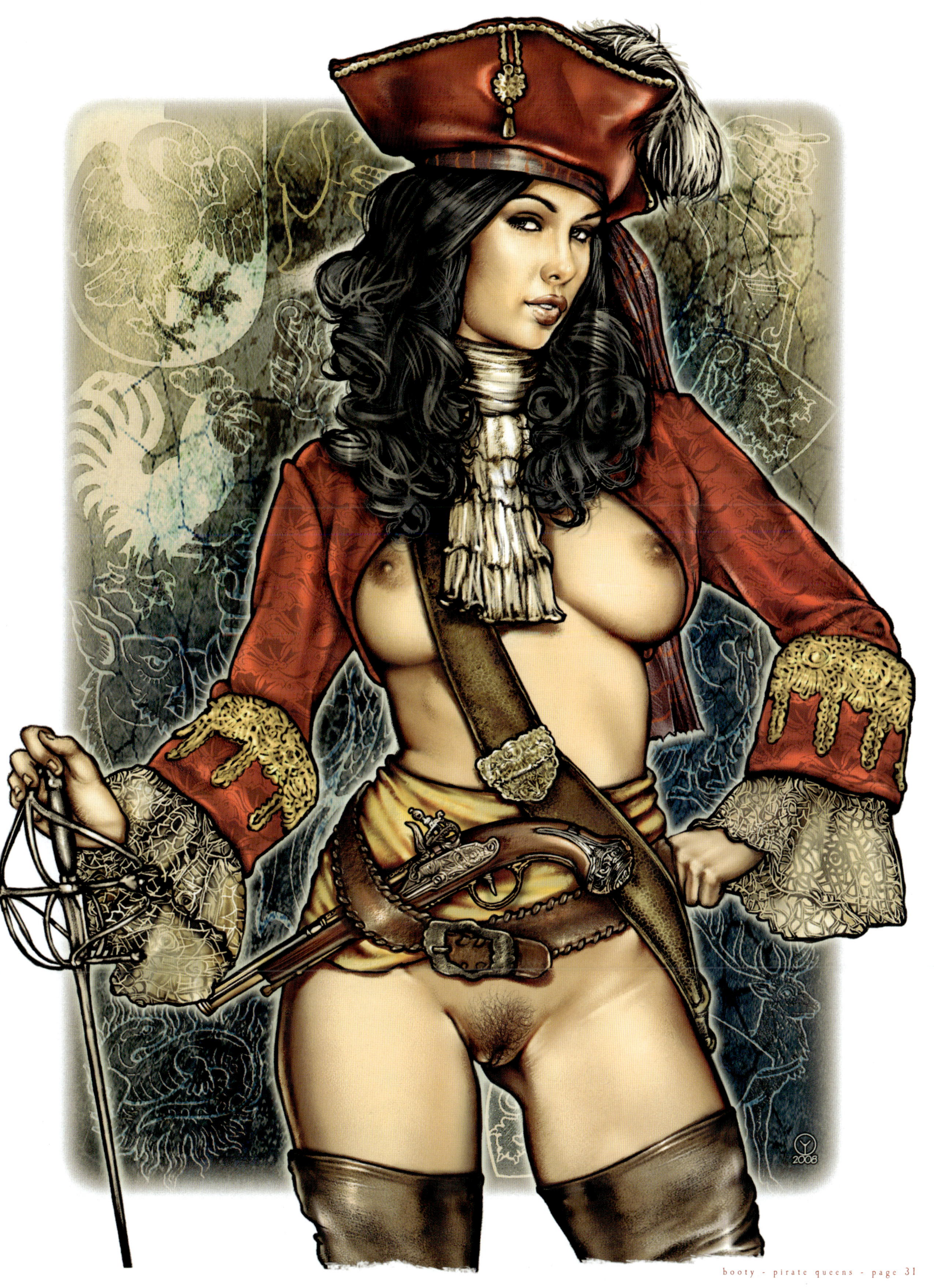
2008

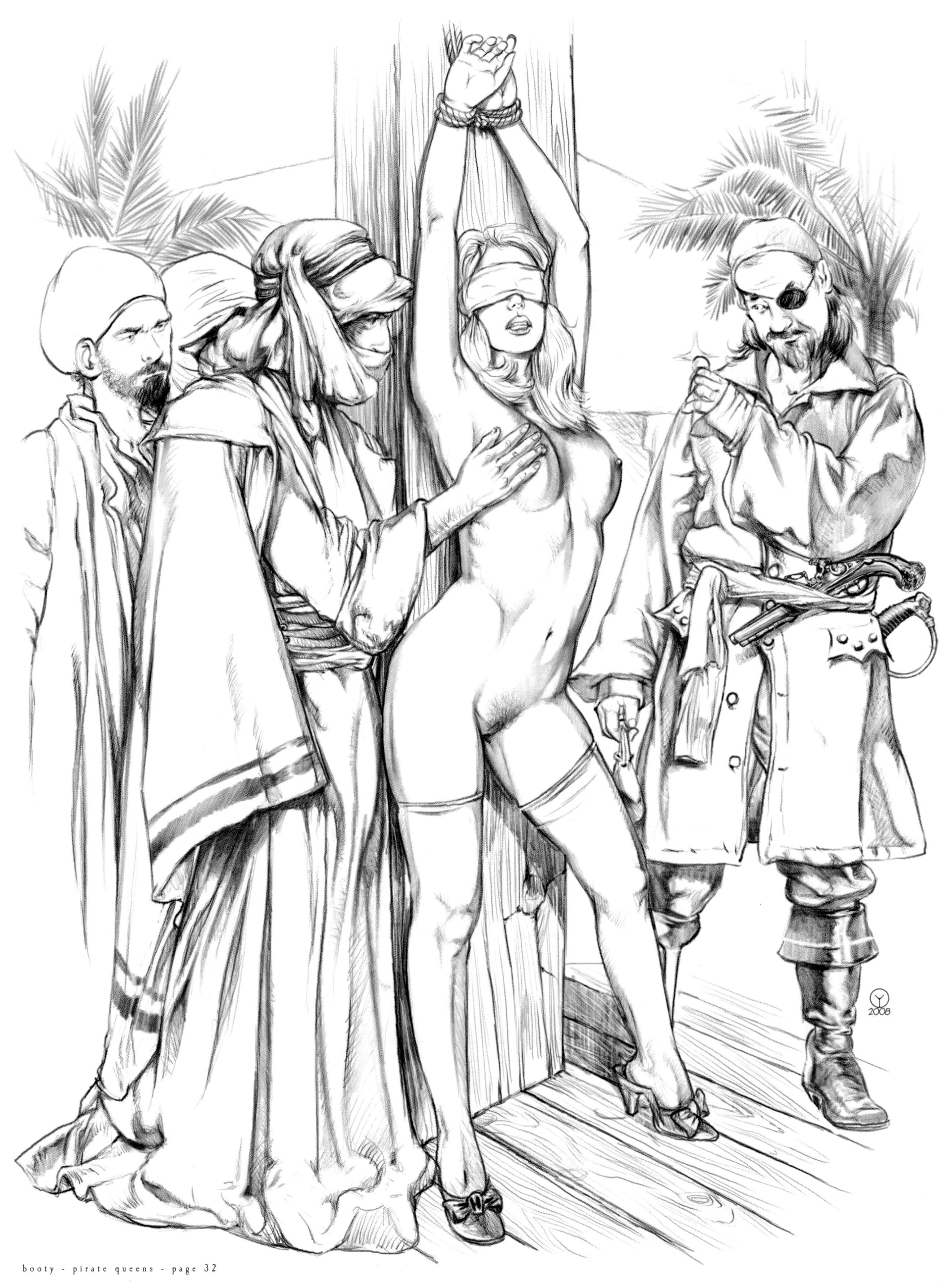

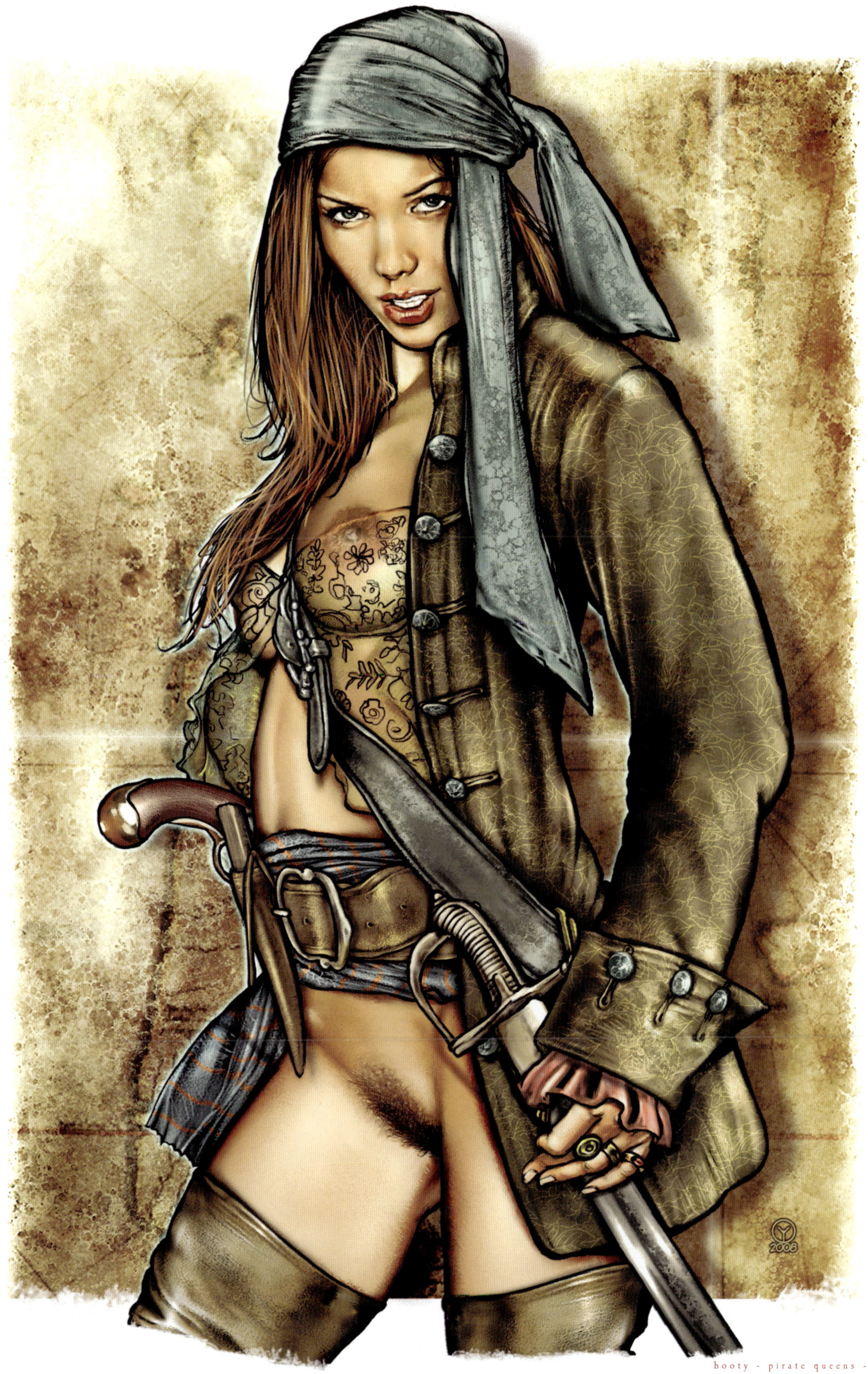
2006

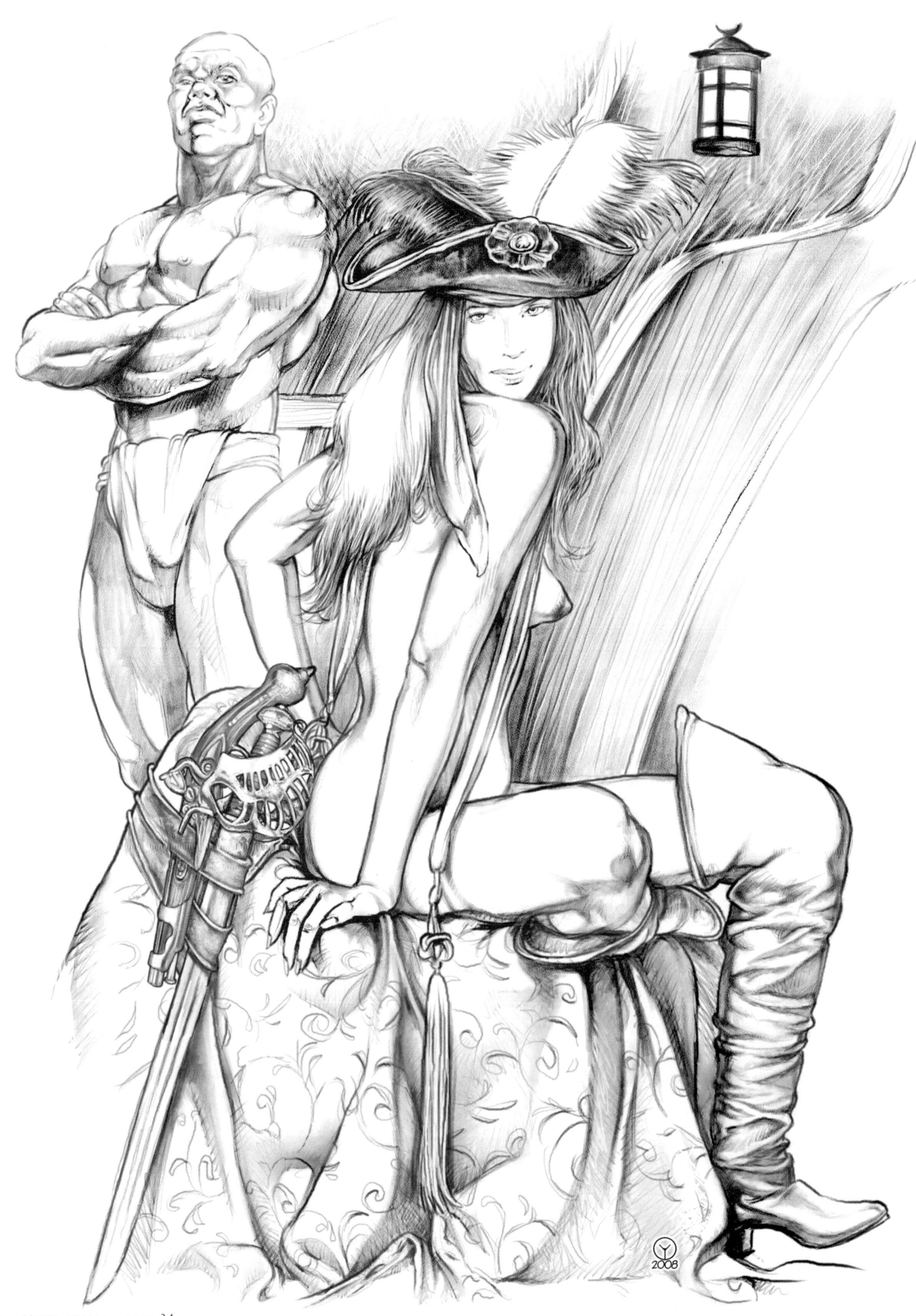
2008

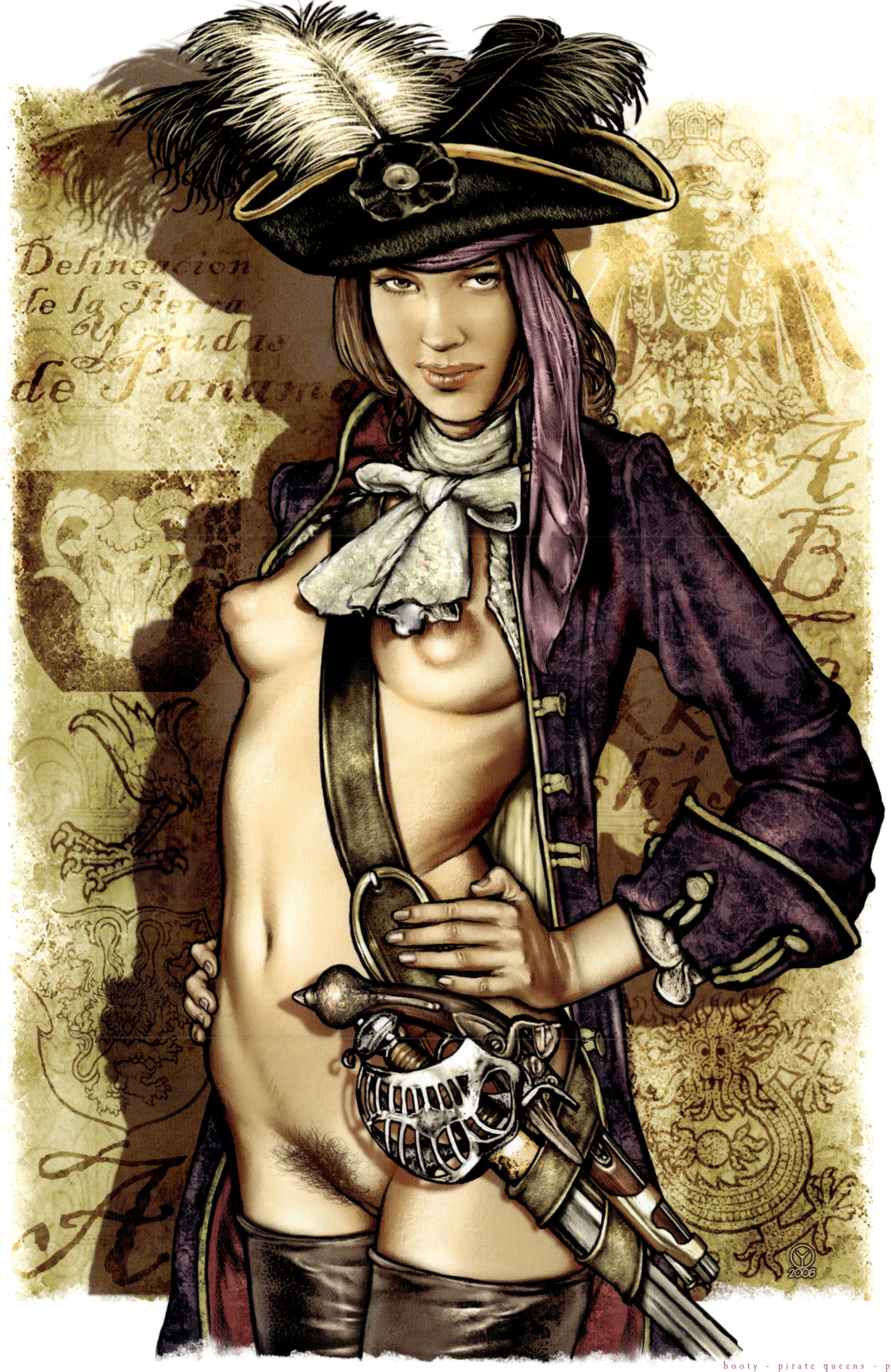
Delineacion
de la Tierra

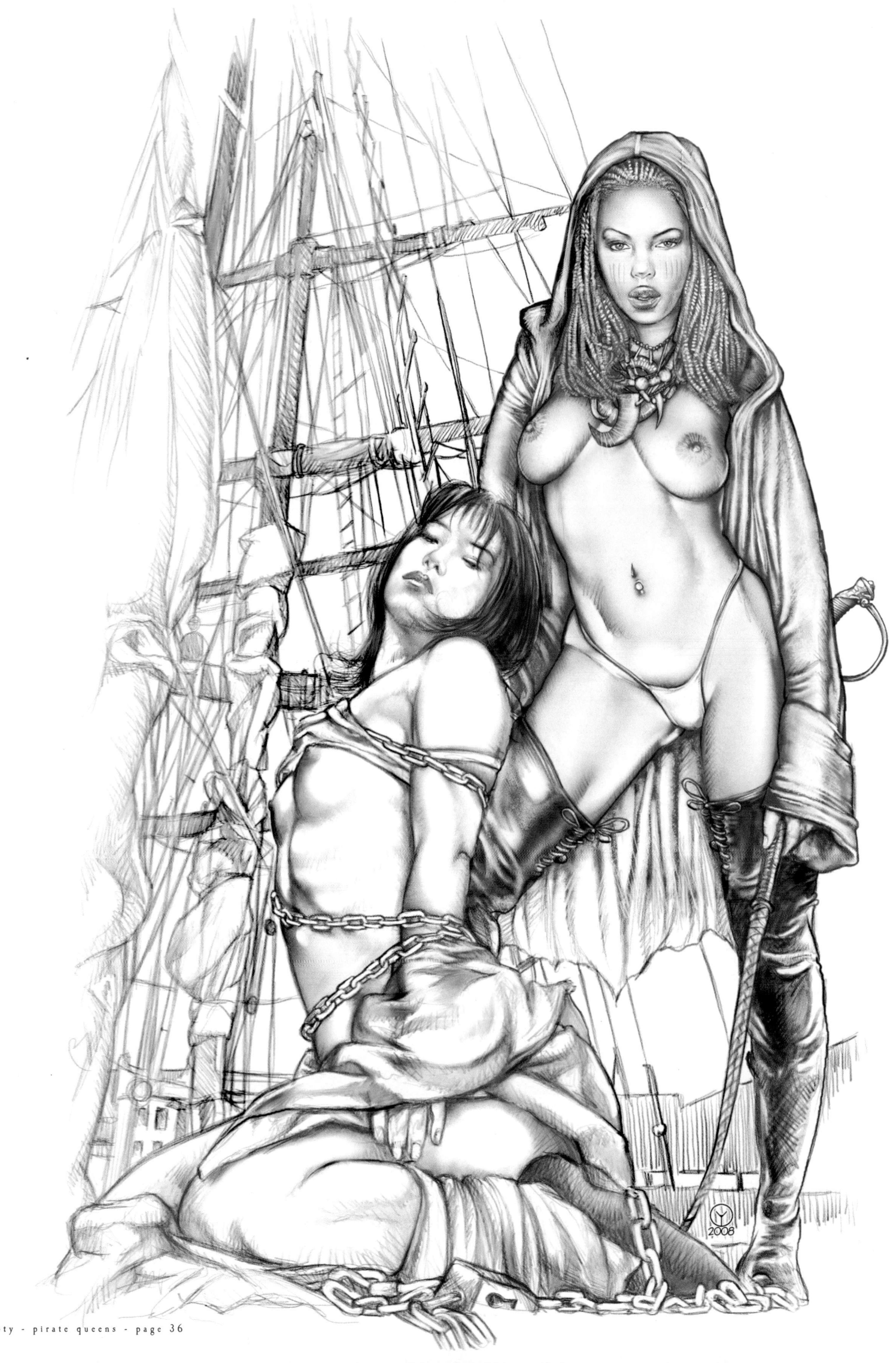

2008

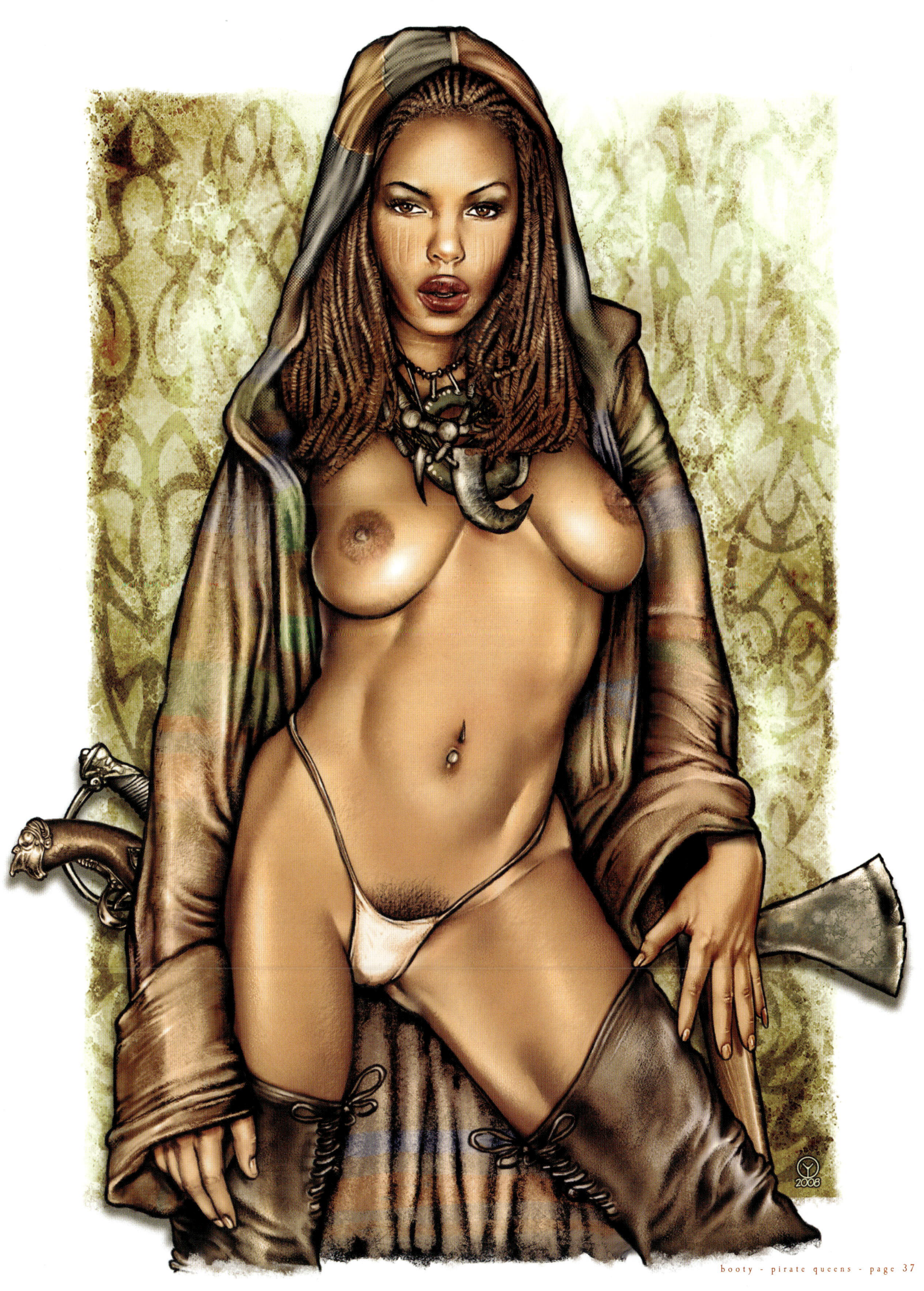

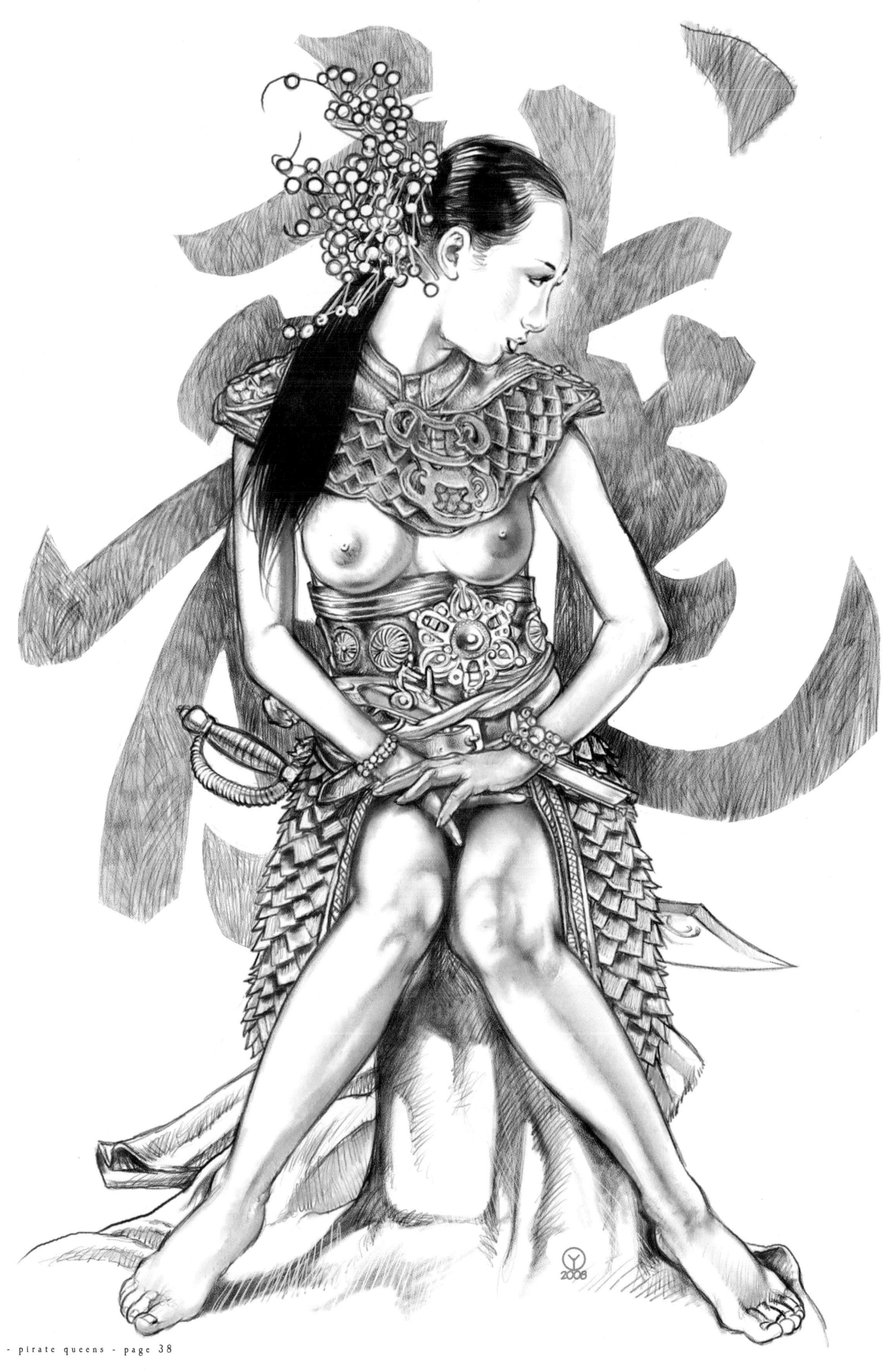

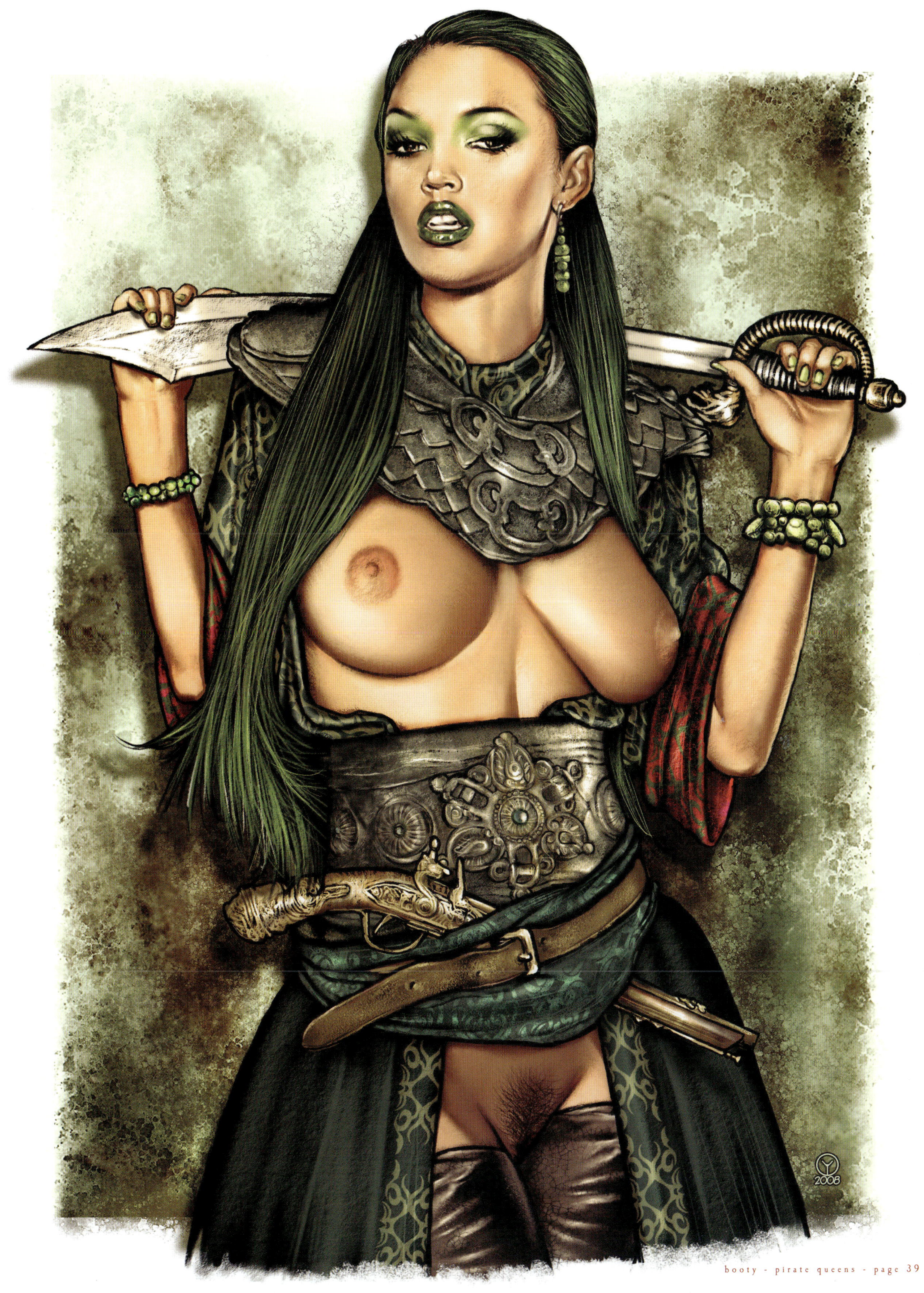

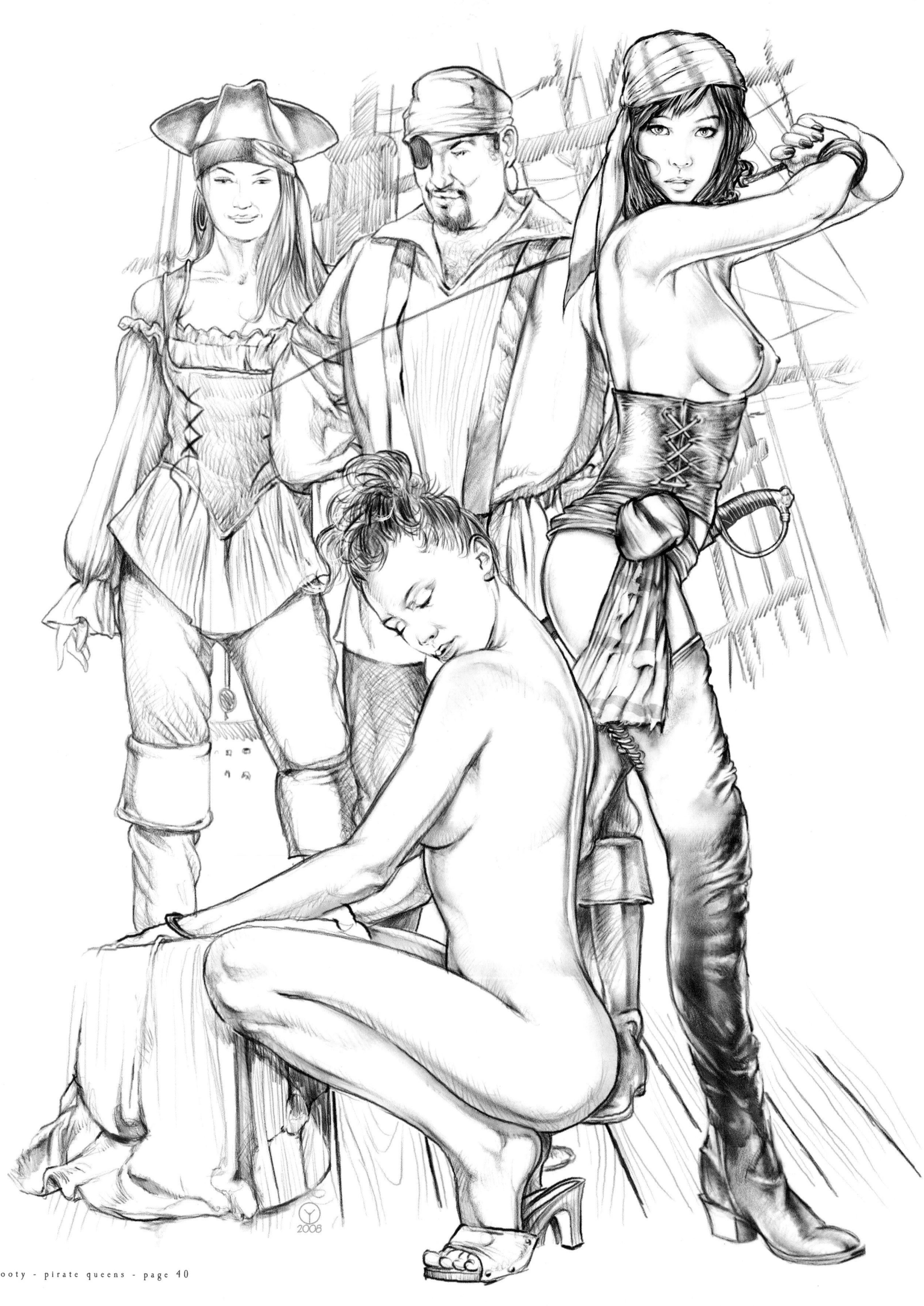

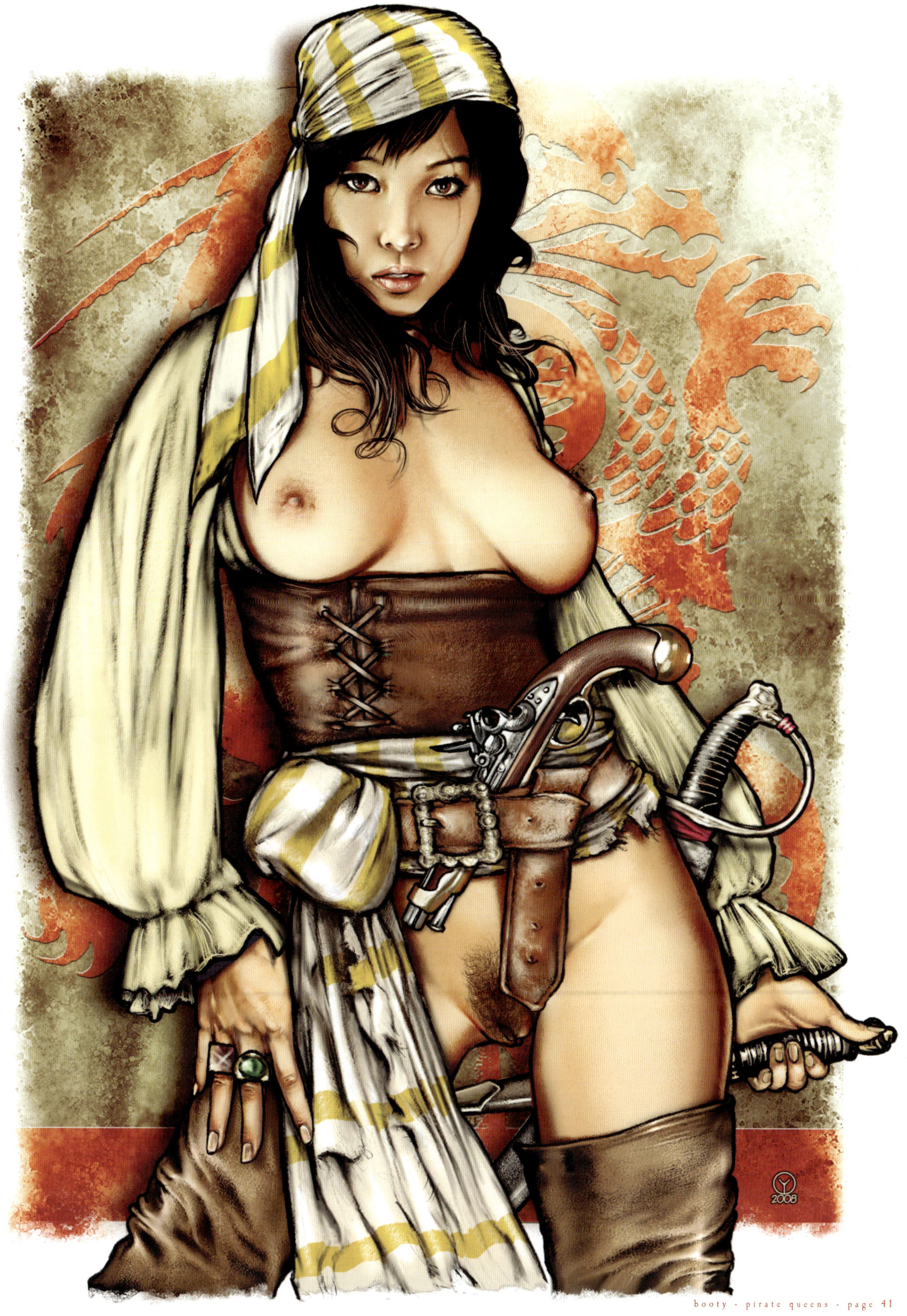
2008

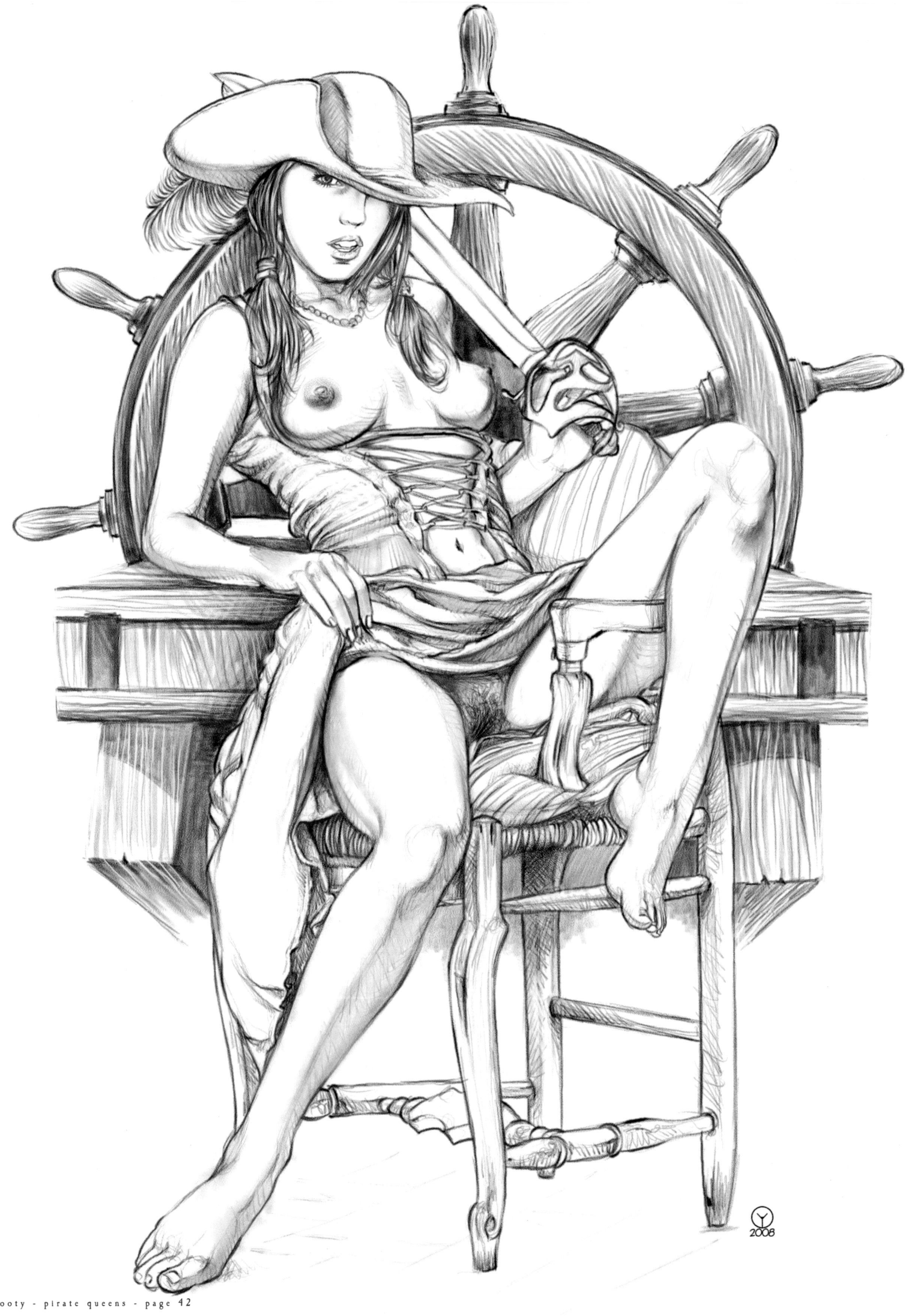

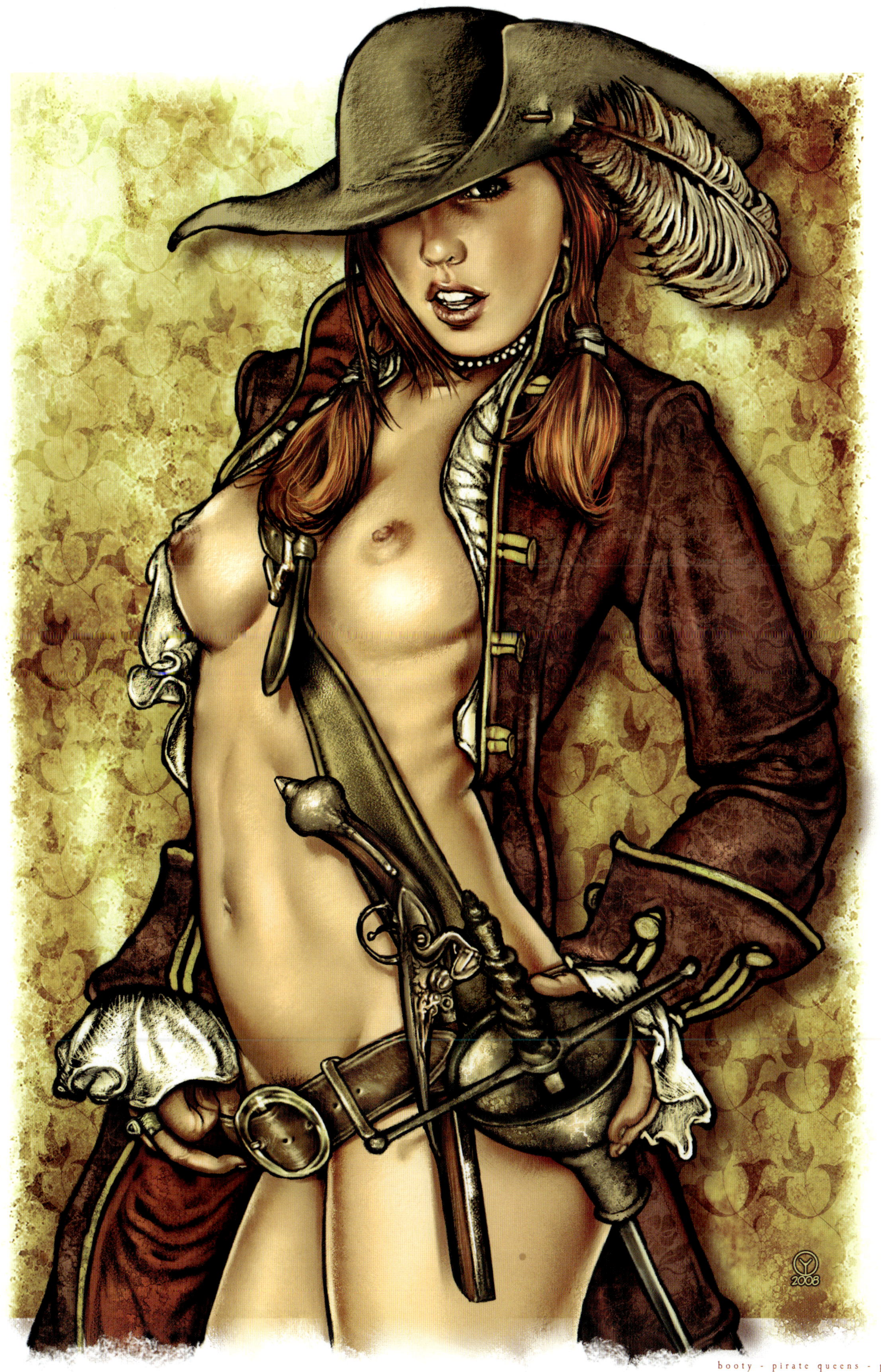
2008

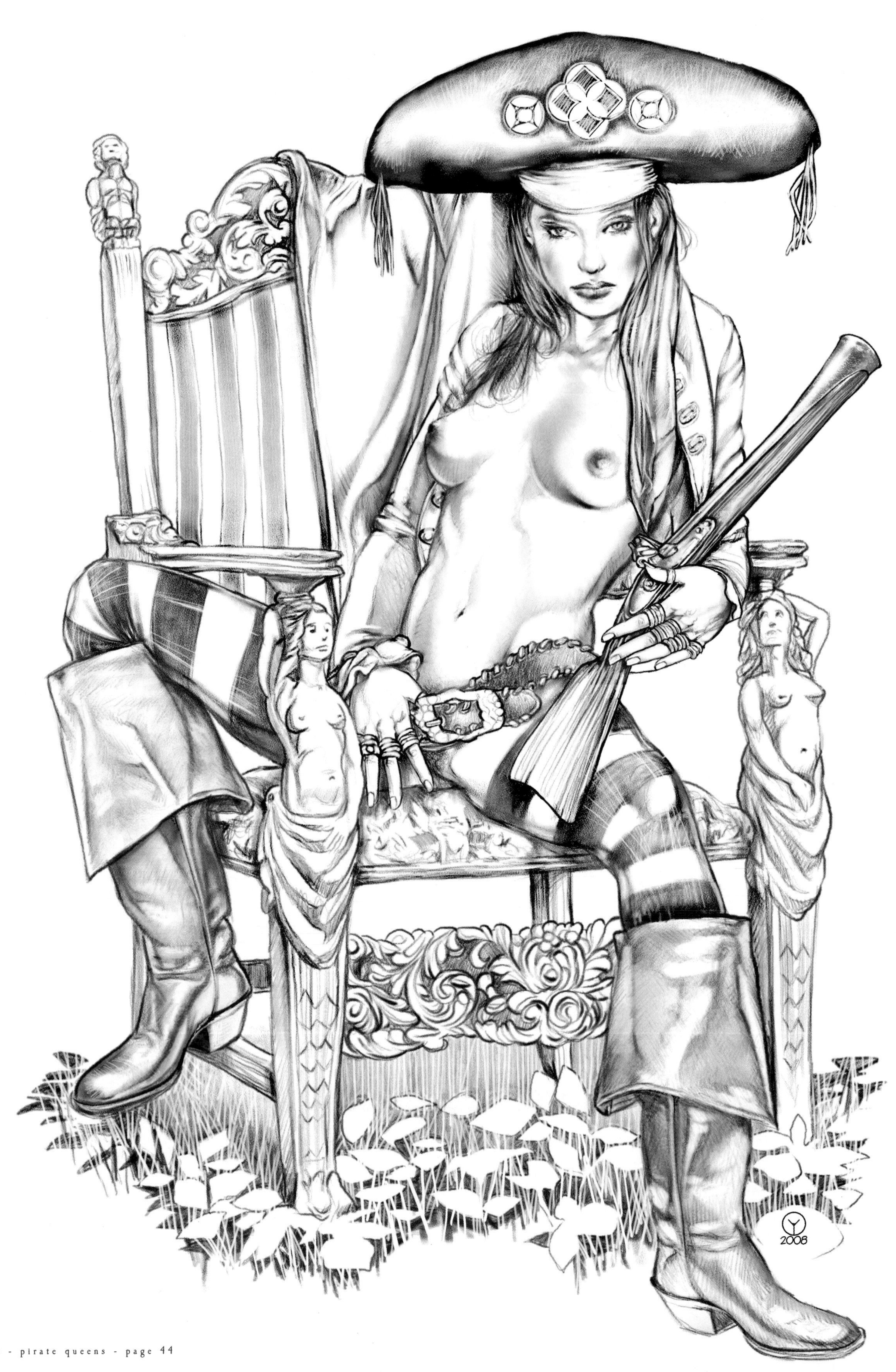
2008

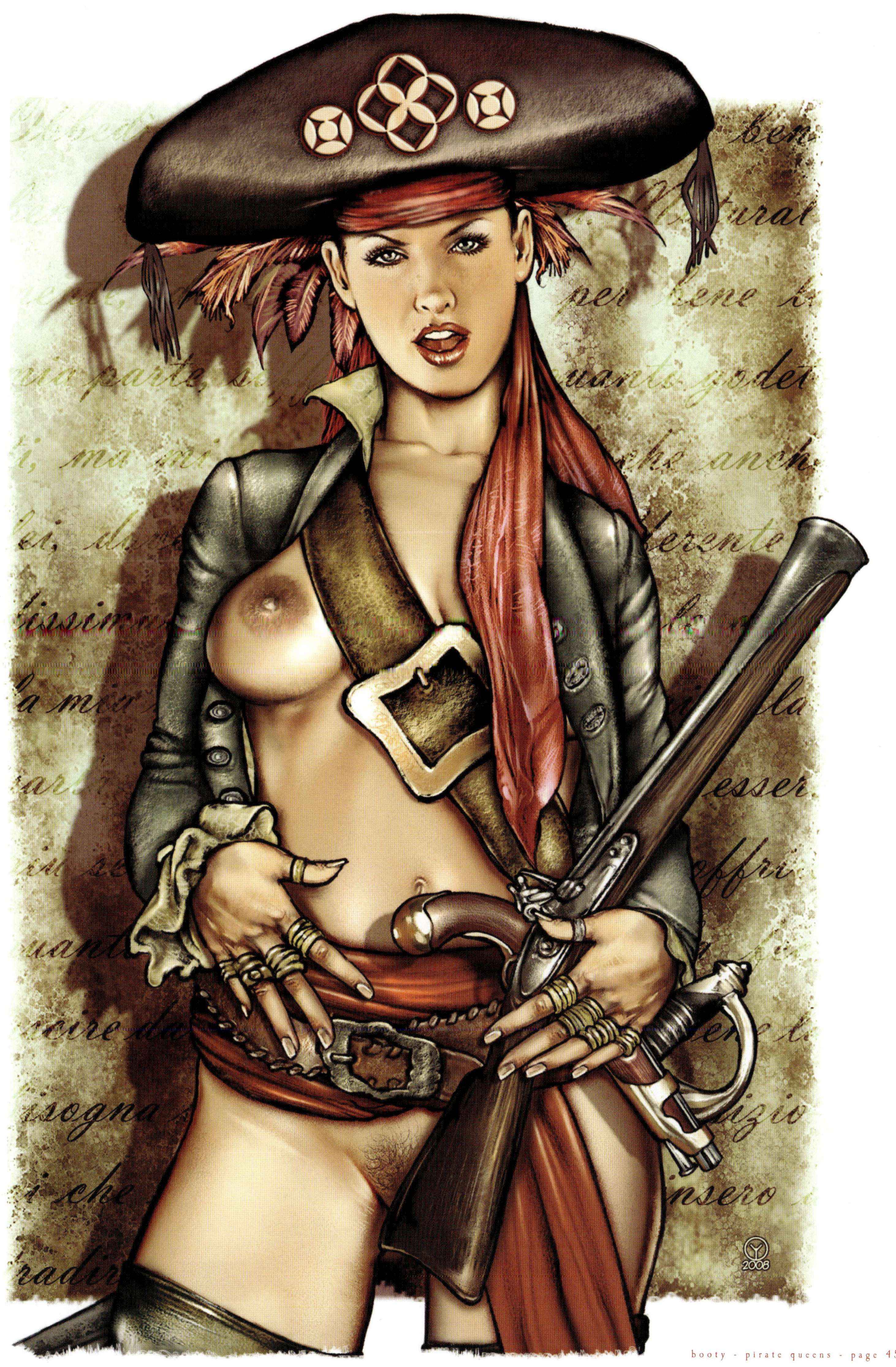

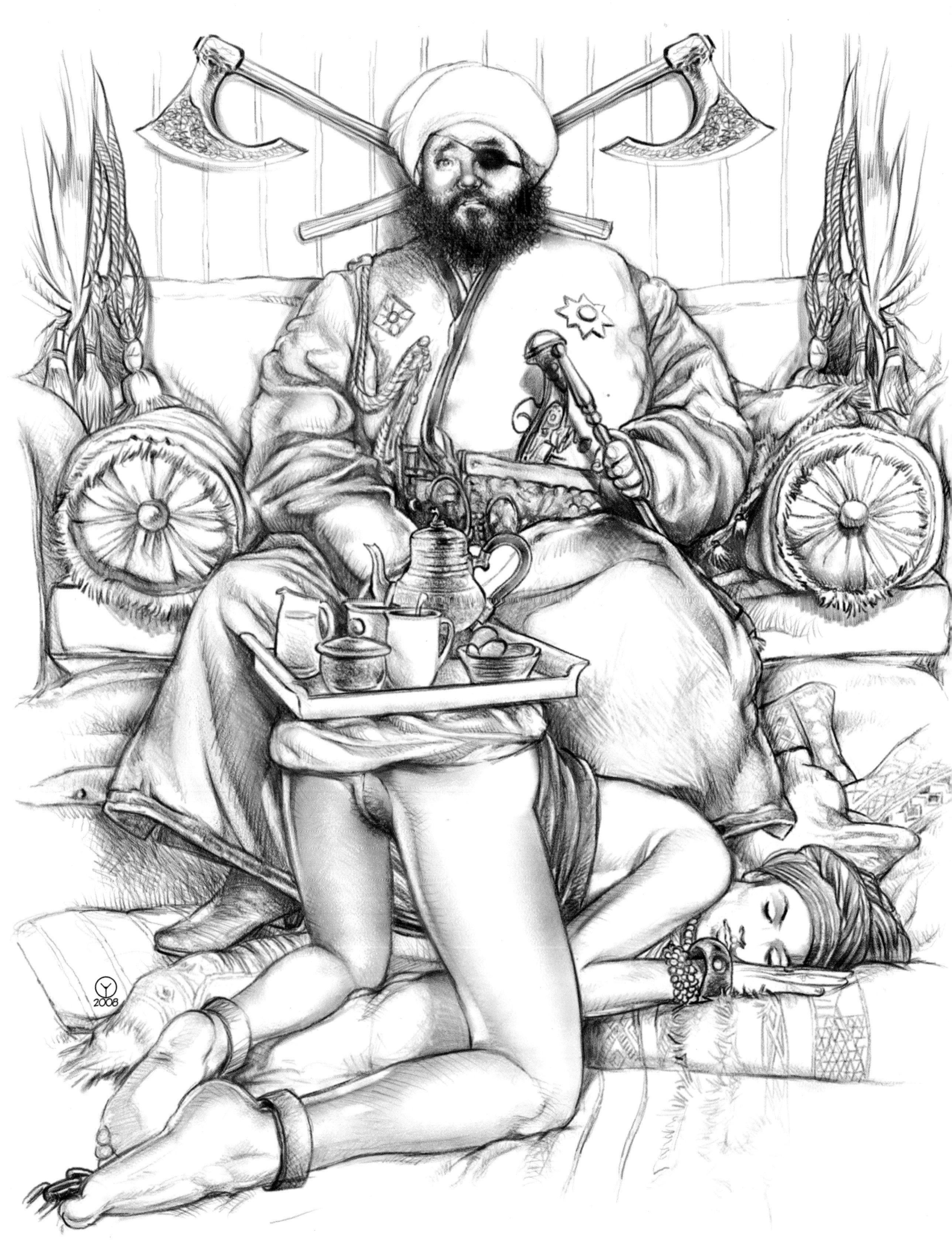
2008

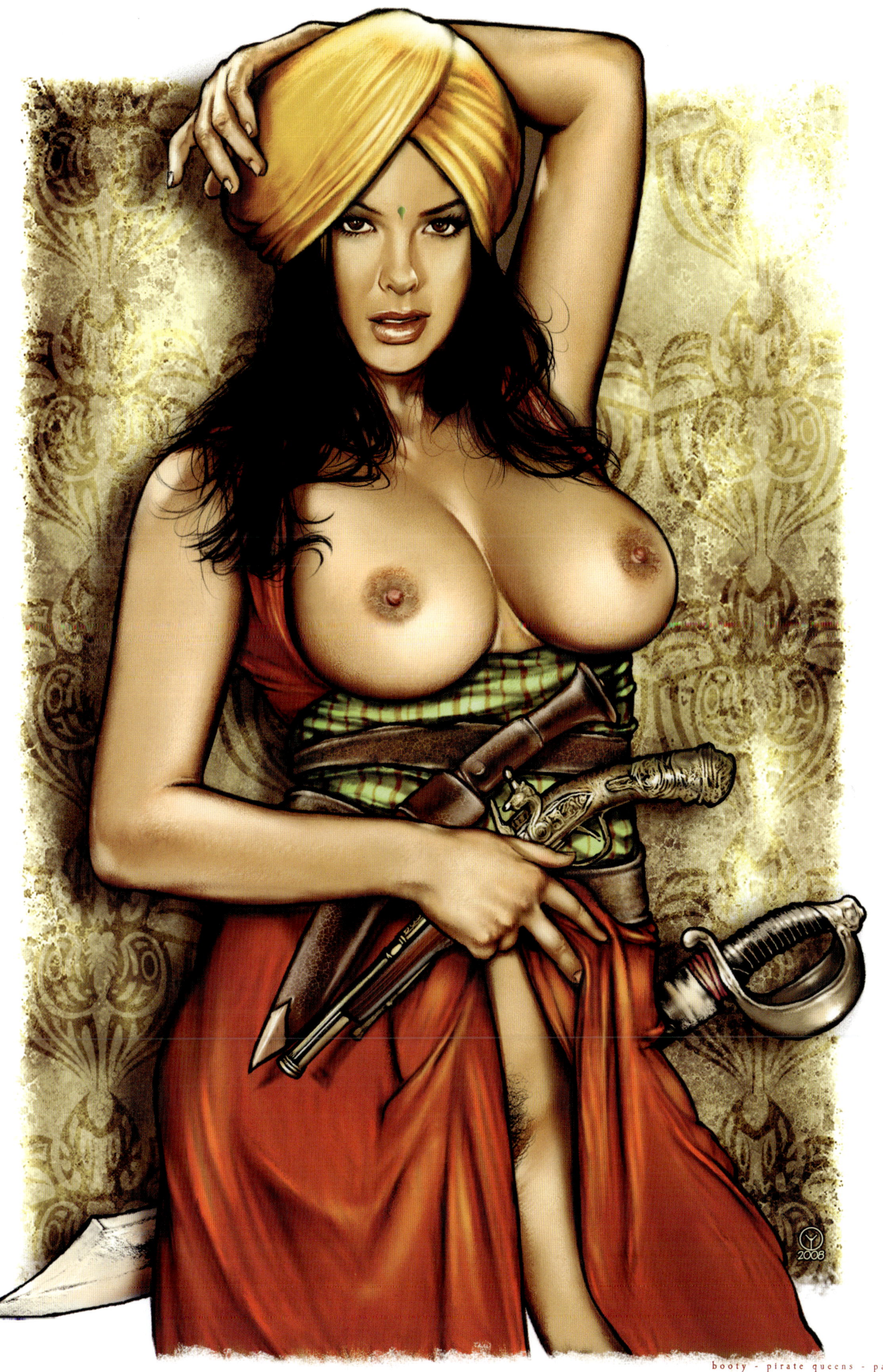

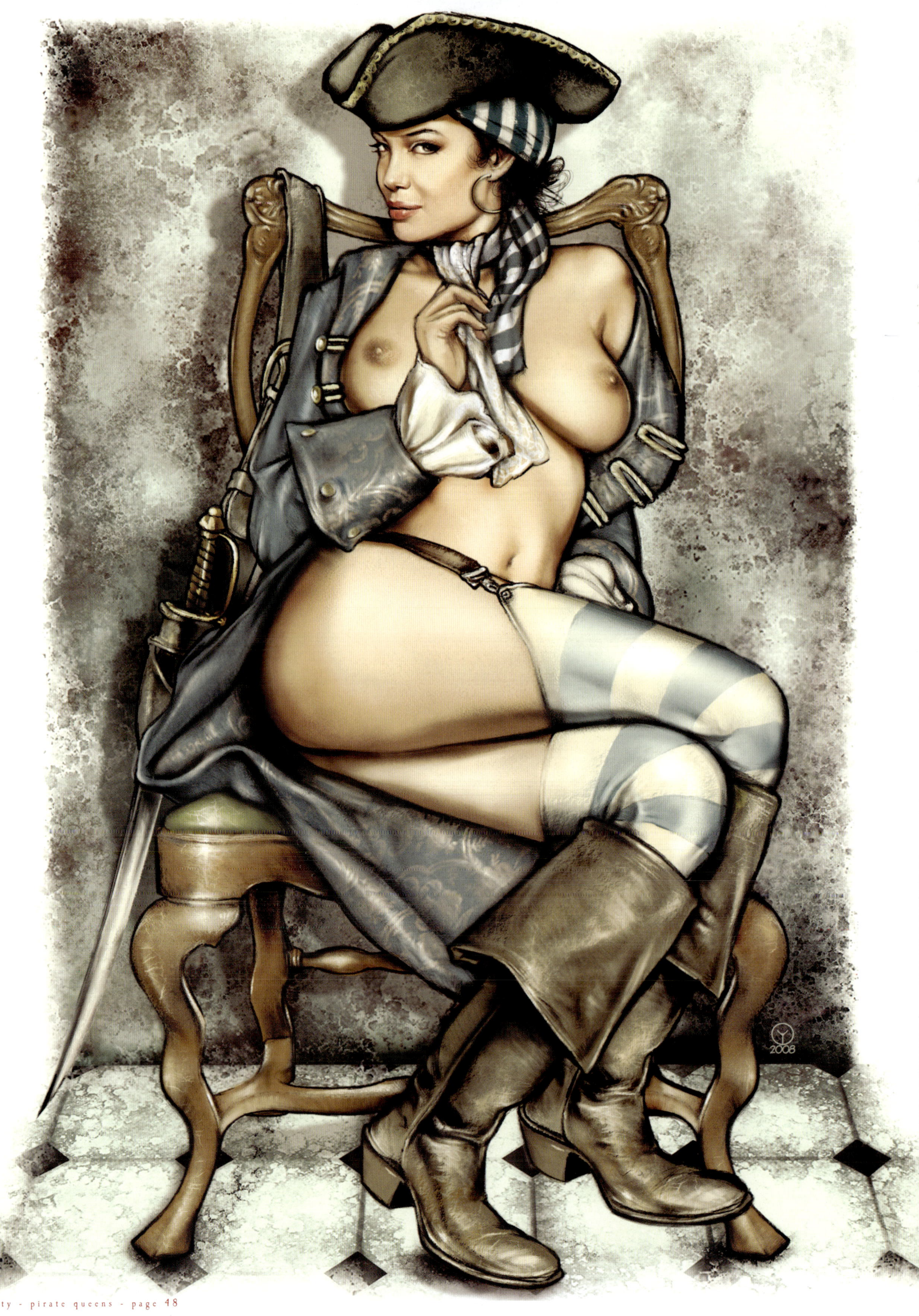
2008